Small Hotels and Inns of Andalucía

Charming Places to Stay
In Southern Spain

Guy Hunter-Watts

SANTANA BOOKS

CREDITS

Small Hotels and Inns of Andalucía is published by:
Ediciones Santana S.L.,
Apartado 422, Fuengirola 29640 (Málaga), Spain.
Tel: 952 485 838.   Fax: 952 485 367.
E-mail: info@santanabooks.com
www.santanabooks.com

First published in September 2001.
Copyright © Guy Hunter-Watts.

Design by Graham Banks for grahamsgraphics.com
Cover design by Tina Bradley.

Map of Andalucía by Estinca Ingeniería Cartográfica.

Printed by Gráficas San Pancracio S.L., Poligono Industrial San
Luis, Calle Orotava 17, Málaga, Spain.

Depósito Legal: MA-1.261/2001   ISBN 84-89954-18-6.

ACKNOWLEDGEMENTS

My first thanks must go to Annie Shillito and Alastair Sawday. I first got to know many of the places that appear in this book when researching their "Special Places to Stay" guide and it has been in no small measure thanks to their creating a book for me to edit that I've been able to survive in Andalucía. When I told them of my plans to write another guide for Santana they generously agreed. I am hugely grateful to them both as colleagues and friends.

Mike "Miguel" Lewin, a man who knows Andalucía like few others, put me on the trail of some great places, Rachel Dring told me about a wonderful new hotel in Tarifa and Barry Birch, one of the funniest men in southern Spain, sent me off to see a seriously good new hotel in Osuna. This book is better thanks to all of your help.

But the biggest thank you goes to Emma for putting up with my long periods away from home and self-imposed exile in the office when I got back.

¡Muchísimas gracias a todos!

ABOUT THE AUTHOR

Guy Hunter-Watts first came to Andalusia in the early eighties, when he cycled across the country on an old push bike. The trip was the inspiration for a return to formal study in the UK after which he taught at a South American university.

He then returned to Spain and, after a year of teaching in Salamanca, headed for the mountains west of Ronda. After setting up home there, he worked in Peru, Mexico and India as a guide before coming home to roost in Montecorto.

He now works as a walking guide, writer and helps run a small B&B.

CONTENTS

INTRODUCTION

The hotel scene in Andalucía is changing fast. The number of visitors to the region increases year after year and although many come for the traditional sun-and-sea fix, more and more of them are beginning to head inland, in search of *tapas* and *fino* rather than Sunday roast and pints of Guinness.

Ten years ago, they would have found it difficult to find consistently good places to stay. True, there have always been the Paradors and they have played an important role in opening visitors' eyes to the beauty of Spain's interior. But however wonderful their setting, they have often been plagued by a job-for-life mentality and a centralised, corporate mentality. Even if standards have improved with the advent of shorter working contracts, you wouldn't automatically think parador nowadays if you were planning a really special break.

Spain's entry into the EEC has set a very different ball in motion. Thanks to a generous programme of subsidies for less developed parts of the Community, a huge change has come about in Andalucía. Several would-be hoteliers have decided to bite the bullet and launch themselves into building the hotel of their dreams – in the assurance that up to 40% of the funding would be coming from Brussels.

The result of this, together with the new vogue for rural tourism, has been a huge increase in the number of decent places to stay in the villages of Andalucía. Where I live, close to Ronda, at least a dozen new places have opened in the space of just five years and nearly every one of them is the sort of place where you would happily lay your head. Go to the remotest village in the provinces of Granada, Malaga or Cádiz and you'll invariably stumble across a recently opened *posada* or *casa rural* where the food is likely to be excellent and where your room will be as comfortable as that of a four star hotel. And it will probably cost half the price.

This book celebrates this new trend. There are more wonderful places to stay at Andalucía than ever before. Many of those included within these pages have only recently opened their doors to their first guests and you'll find them in no other guide.

OUR CRITERIA FOR INCLUDING PLACES

When researching this guide, I visited many more places than those that were eventually included. The fact that some failed to make it into these pages is no reflection on their professionalism. They were simply places that I might not stay at given other choices in the area. This is bound to be a subjective decision but I hope that I've developed an idea of what might appeal to most readers.

You'll find hotels and B&Bs for all tastes and all budgets in this book. The bottom line for my including a place is that it must be clean, friendly, comfortable, in a good location and exceptional in some way or another. Just what constitutes "exceptional" can vary enormously. It might be the building itself, the views from the terrace, the peacefulness (always high on my personal check list) or the proximity to, say, the Mezquita in Cordoba or the Alhambra in Granada. Read the text carefully and you should be able to see why I like a particular place and of any misgivings, if any, I feel about it. There is, after all, no such thing as hotel perfection.

USING THIS GUIDE

PAGE NUMBERS

The hotels are grouped by provinces – there are eight in
Andalucía – and have been numbered on a west to east basis,
beginning with Huelva and ending with Almeria. The flagged
number on the map corresponds to the actual page number of
the hotel. You'll find the number of the map on which any hotel
is flagged indicated on its page in the book.

ADDRESSES

Occasionally the address that appears in the book is the hotel's
postal address and not that of the hotel itself. When you come
to visiting a place simply follow instructions in the
"directions"section and you should have no problem finding it.

PHONE/FAX NUMBERS

Self explanatory. Remember that some places with the same
phone and fax number need to switch the fax on to receive your
message. So you may have to request this first, by phone. Any
number beginning with a 6 is that of a mobile phone.

E-MAIL/WEB PAGES

More and more hotels are using e-mail and this is often the
quickest way of getting a confirmation of availability. It also
makes it faster and easier for a hotel to send you further
information. A hotel's web site can, of course, give you a great
deal more information than we can in this guide and is always
worth a quick visit to the web site, especially if you are planning
a stay of several nights

DESCRIPTION

Remember that this is my personal assessment of a place and I
make no apologies for this. It might differ in some way to
yours. Please let me know (see the form at the end of this book)
if you disagree with anything or if you think that anything is
missing from the description.

ROOMS

We have tried to make it clear what the exact bed configuration is of any hotel. Occasionally hotels differ over what they describe as a suite. Some see it as a large bedroom with enough space for a couple of easy chairs and/or a sofa (also sometimes referred to as a "junior" suite, whilst for others the term is only used if there is a completely separate lounge. If the latter is important to you, then check at the time of booking.

PRICES - Important!

Because this book will span both the end of 2001 and the whole of 2002, we have quoted prices in both pesetas and euros. Some of us, at least, will take a while to adjust, so we felt that you should have both prices, side by side. Remember that the prices we quote are those of 2001. If you are using this book after then, be prepared for a small increase in the prices quoted. But it would be unusual for these to have gone up by more than 10%. Many will stay the same or will have been rounded just slightly up (or down) into a whole number of euros.

MEALS

Breakfast - Any of you who have lived in Spain for any length of time will know that breakfast here is often a rather meagre affair. In many hotels the standard offering is just toast and jam with coffee or tea. Fresh orange juice is becoming more common but don't automatically expect it. Be aware, too, that breakfast often doesn't get going in some places until 9am. If you need to get on the road before then, you'd be best to pay your bill the night before.

Lunch/Dinner - The price that we have quoted in the book for meals is generally that of the set menu or, occasionally when there is not one available, the average price that you'd expect to pay for a three course meal. Be aware that waiters often don't automatically tell you what's available on the set menu, so always ask (¿hay menu del dia?). And also be aware that dining a la carte can often be two or three times more expensive than going for the set meal. We have included the dates/days of the week when some places close their restaurants. Always check when booking that food will be available to avoid disappointment.

DIRECTIONS

Again, I hope, largely self explanatory. To make navigation easier, it's always worth having a copy of the Michelin map of Andalucía, no 446, along with you. The space that we have for describing how to find any given place is limited. Many hotels will happily fax/e-mail you more detailed route notes/maps for finding them.

STAR RATINGS

We haven't listed these in this book. I've stayed at five star hotels that have less character than the average house brick, and at one star hotels "that would be fit for a king". On this subject one of the hoteliers in this book said to me "The stars are in the sky". I couldn't agree more.

EXPLANATION OF SYMBOLS

(YES)	Owners/staff speak English
(JA)	Owners/staff speak German
♿	Hotel has room(s) with full handicapped facilities (see 1)
❄	Bedrooms have air-conditioning
🏊	Hotel has its own swimming pool
🐕	Pets are accepted, regardless of size (see 2)
(V)	Vegetarian food can be prepared (see 3)
💳	Credit Cards are accepted
🚶	Good walks close to the hotel
🪑	Garden/patio area where guests can sit outside
👪	Hotel is suitable/caters for young children (see 4)
🚗	Hotel has its own car park (see 5)

NOTES
Always check on exact facilities if you are handicapped because house rules can vary. Some hotels allow dogs in rooms, other only in purpose-built kennels. Always check. If you have special dietary requirements, let the hotel know prior to your arrival. Check before you arrive what exactly is available in the way of cots, baby-sitter etc. Some city-centre hotels' car parks aren't adjacent to the hotel, so it's worth checking before you arrive.

GENERAL HOTEL INFORMATION

REGISTRATION

Spanish Law still requires that you should register on arrival at any hotel in Spain. This can seem like an ordeal when you arrive after a long drive but remember that this is as tedious for hotel staff as it is for you. Once a hotel has noted down the details of your passport, they have no right to keep hold of it.

BOOKING / CREDIT CARDS

Be aware that it is common practice amongst larger hotels to ask for a credit card number when you make a reservation by phone or by email. Standard practice is to charge the cost of the first night against your card. This is generally a non-refundable deposit. According to Spanish law a hotel shouldn't debit your card for more than the cost of one night for every ten booked.

Some people are wary of giving card details over the phone. But you should know that to date I've never heard of a case of fraud and that many hotels operate in this way because of the number of no-shows, particularly common with weekend tourism. When the weather turns bad, that trip to the country can suddenly seem a whole lot less attractive. Remember, too, that many of the smaller, B&B-type places in this guide don't accept payment by credit card. We include a symbol to let you know about those that do or don't take plastic

ARRIVAL / DEPARTURE TIMES

Some hotels have a policy of holding rooms (with or without a credit card information) until a certain time – normally about 8pm – and then letting the room if you haven't shown up by then. So if you're running late, be sure to give a quick call and let the hotel know that you are still coming. And remember that in Spain, as in other countries, most hotels require you to vacate your room by 12am. If you want to leave later, most hotels will be happy to look after your luggage.

HEATING

Most of Andalucia's hotels have been designed primarily with keeping cool in mind. Anybody who has lived for long in southern Spain will know that winters can be wet and cold. If you're headed for one of the more simple places included here, it can be well worth reminding the hotel of your e.t.a., and requesting that radiators should be turned on before you get there. Those same marble floors that are so pleasant in summer can be an ordeal in winter, so pack a pair of thick socks or slippers.

NOISE

You may not be aware of the fact that the Spanish ear is subject to a higher decibel onslaught than any other ear in Europe! Anyone living in Spain will be aware of the Spaniards' love of getting together in large groups and eating and drinking into the early hours. Hotels are, by nature, places where you're likely to come across people who are in party mode and two o'clock in the morning is still early by Friday/Saturday night standards. So if you're a light sleeper ask for a quiet room at the time of booking and be aware that many of the grander cortijo style places are often used for wedding parties at weekends.

NAVIGATING IN THE CITY CENTRES

Córdoba, Granada and Sevilla and some of the larger towns in Andalucía can be really tricky places to negotiate when it comes to finding your hotel. Remember that nearly all hotels charge 2000-2500 pesetas for using their car parks so, it can save you a huge amount of hassle to simply leave your car at any city centre car park and then take a taxi to your hotel. If the amount of baggage you have with you makes this awkward, it can be well worth stopping a taxi and asking the driver to lead you to your hotel. It can save you masses of time and heartache and it would be rare to clock up more than 1000 pesetas in fares.

YOUR OPINION/RECOMMENDATIONS

You may well have your own favourite hotel that doesn't appear in this guide. Please let us know about any place which you think should get a mention and also if you feel that any of our listings doesn't match up to your expectations. With your feed back, this guide will improve with each subsequent edition.

I especially would welcome your comments about your gastronomic experiences. When I visit I can only sample one dish, so it can be difficult to get the "big picture". Please let me know of any particular hits (or misses) and also of any wines that you've really enjoyed. Many thanks.

MAPS
SECTION

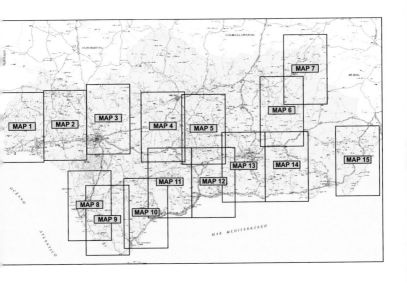

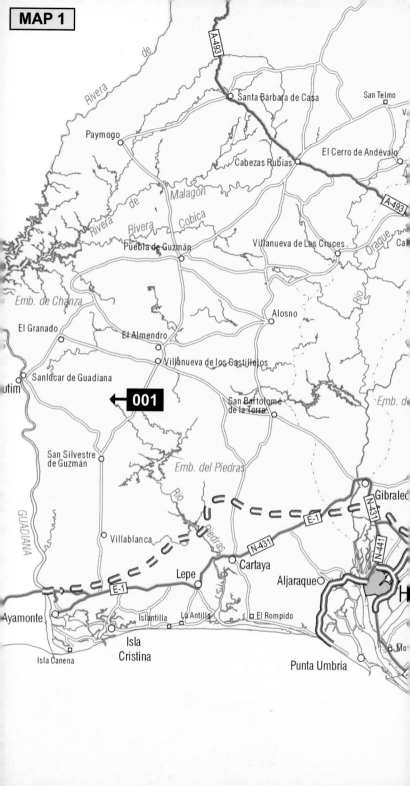

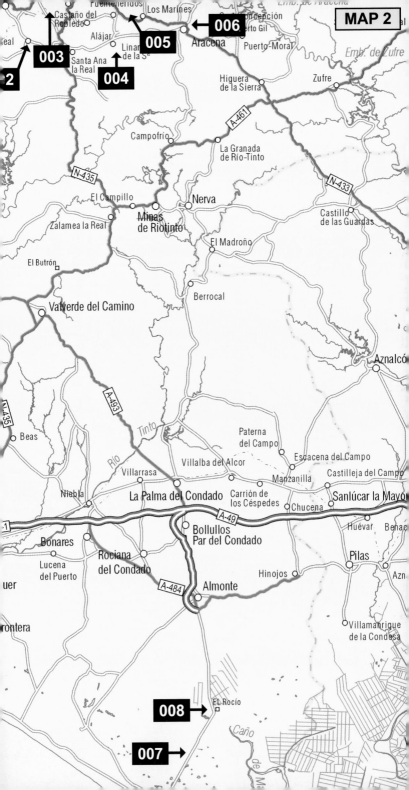

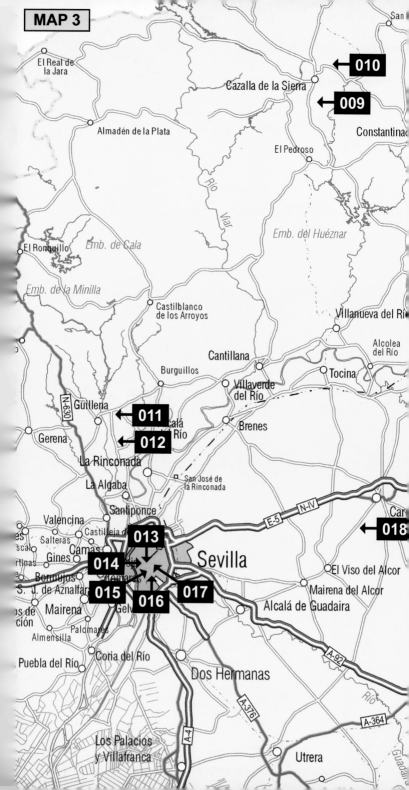

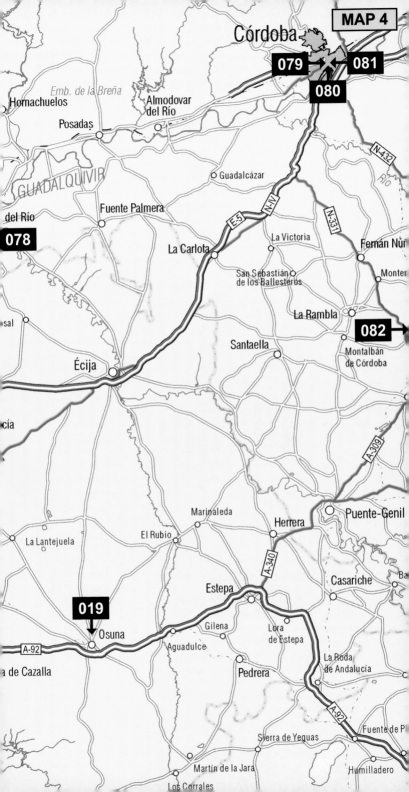

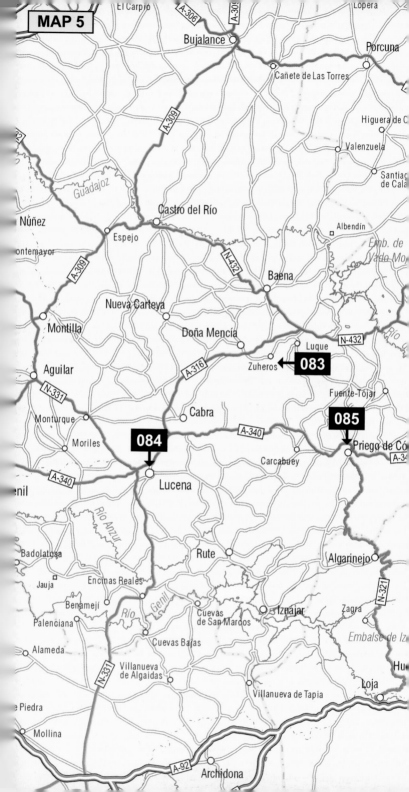

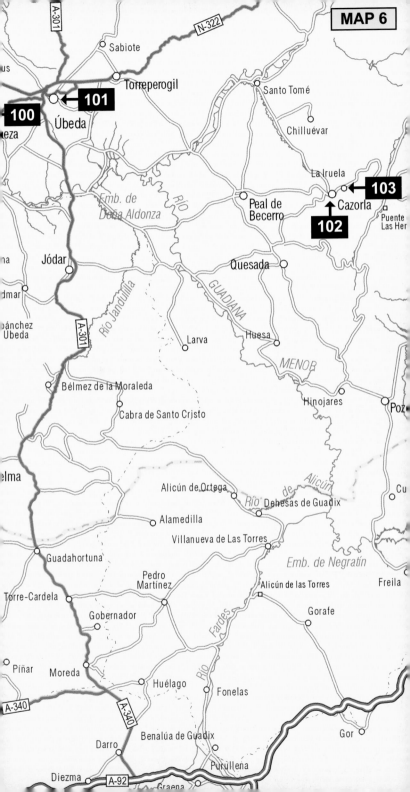

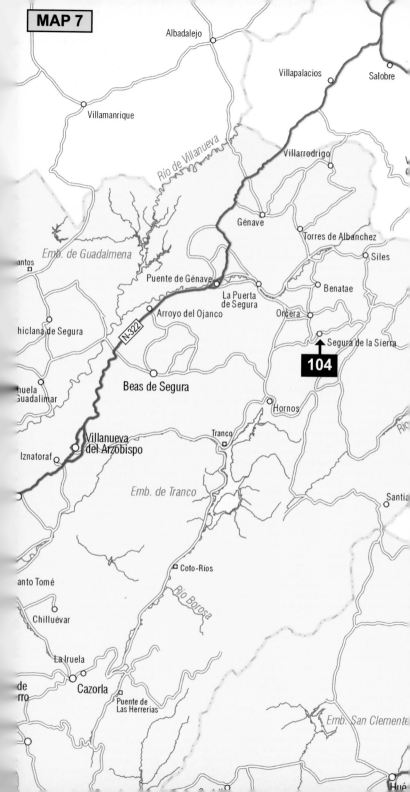

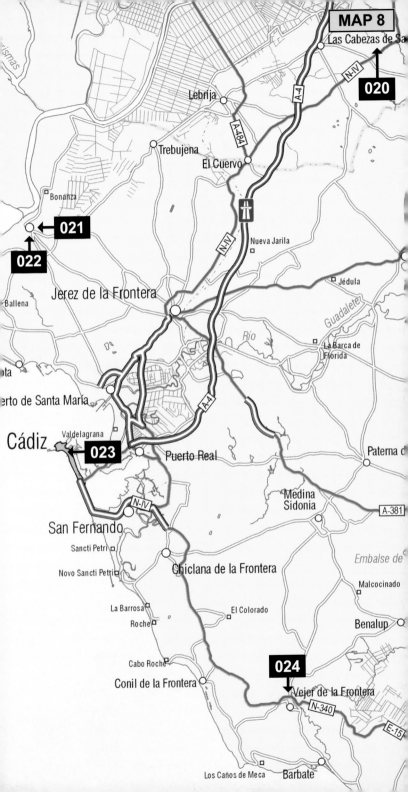

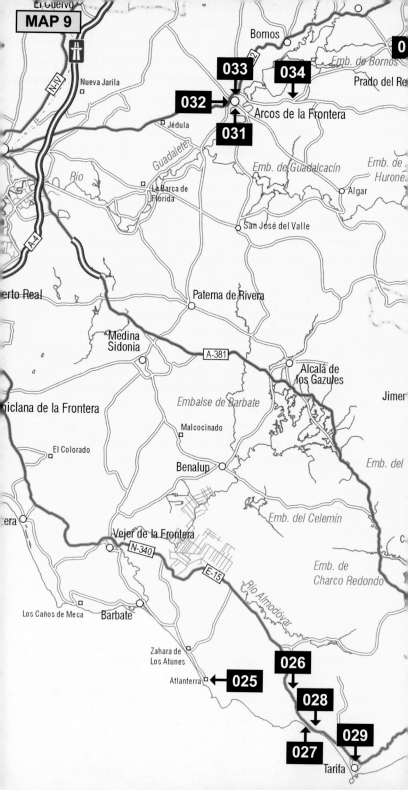

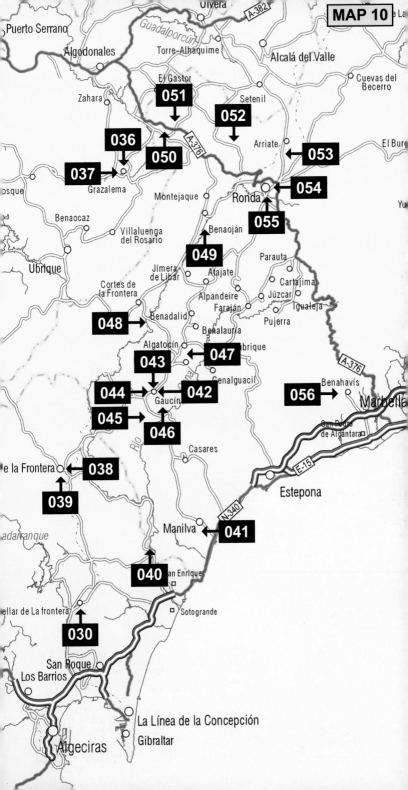

MAP 10

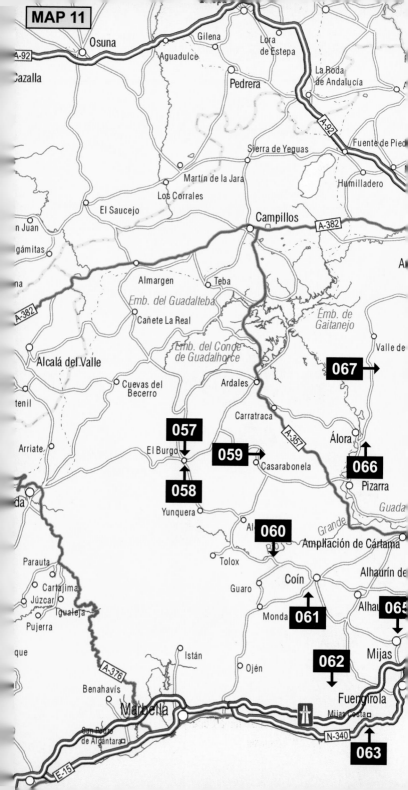

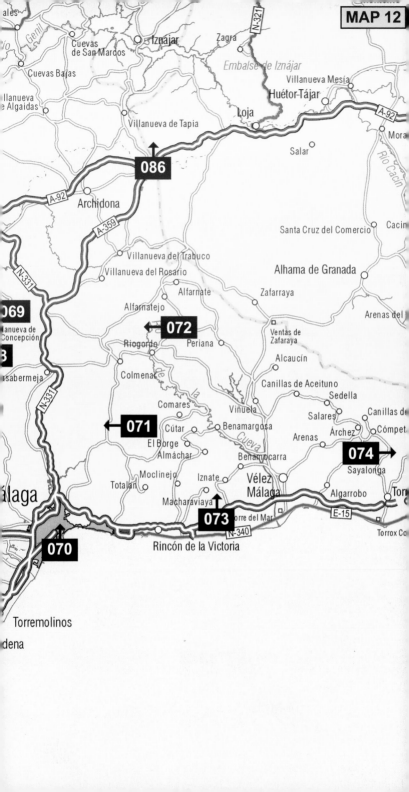

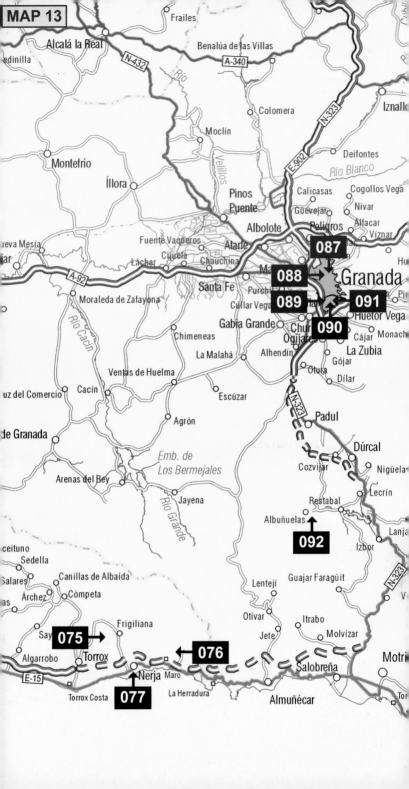

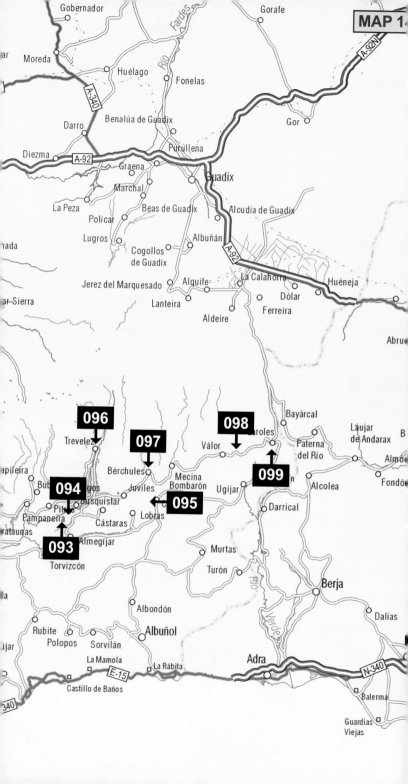

HUELVA
PROVINCE

Hotels 1 to 8

HOTEL-CORTIJO LOS MILLARES

Ctra Ayamonte-Villanueva de los C. km 22.5   **Map: 1**
21540 Villanueva de los Castillejos (Huelva)

Tel: 959 485411 or 959 485407 **Fax:** 959 485410

e-mail: hotel_cortijo@losmillares.com

Closed: August.

Bedrooms: 1 Single, 4 Doubles, 12 Twins, 6 Doubles with lounge and 1 Apartment.

Prices: Single €67 (11200 Ptas), Double/Twin €84–102 (14000– 17000 Ptas), Double with lounge €102 (17000 Ptas), Apartment sleeping four €168 (28000 Ptas) + 7% TAX.

Meals: Breakfast included, Lunch/Dinner €12 (2000 Ptas) including wine.

Getting there: from Sevilla take motorway of 5° Centenario towards Portugal. Exit for Gibraleón then take A-495 to San Bartolomé then A-490 to Villanueva de los Castillejos. There take A-499 towards Ayamonte and after approx. 8km turn right and follow track to Los Millares.

Management: Inés María Deleyto Gómez

Los Millares is a *latifundio* (very large farm), a reminder of a bygone age when being in the right place at the right moment during the Reconquest could mean being rewarded with a tract of land the size of an English county. This vast estate, stretching all the way to the Portuguese border, is yours to explore on foot, by bike, on horseback or in the back of a 4-wheel drive. This is a land of oak forest and dense Mediterranean scrub, of streams, rivers and reservoirs that teem with fish (rods, lines and sinkers are all provided by your hosts). Hunting has always been a part of life here and every last corner of this old farmhouse is adorned with trophies, skins and other hunting memorabilia/paraphernalia. Not, perhaps, a place for vegetarians. Most bedrooms and bathrooms are cavernous and have views out to the gardens and, beyond, to the vast estate. The strutting peacocks, at least, have been spared the bullet and – out of hunting season – a stay here would be deeply relaxing. And the set meals are marvellous value.

To see and do: visit to Sanlúcar de Guadiana, day trip to Portugal, walking and riding.

CASA GARCÍA

Avenida de San Martín 2
21350 Almonaster la Real
(Huelva)

Map: 2

Tel: 959 143109 **Fax:** 959 143109

Closed: Never.

Bedrooms: 3 Doubles, 18 Twins and 1 Suite.

Prices: Double/Twin €42 (7000 Ptas), Suite €72–78 (12000–13000 Ptas) + 7% TAX.

Meals: Breakfast €2–3 (250–500 Ptas), Lunch/Dinner €20–30 (3500–5000 Ptas) excluding wine.

Getting there: from Aracena take the N-433 towards Portugal. Shortly before reaching Cortegana turn left to Almonaster. Casa García is on the right at the entrance to the village.

Management: Juan García Portero

Almonaster la Real is one of the loveliest of a string of mountain villages which stretch west through the Aracena Park towards the Portuguese border. Walking the old paths which link these places feels rather like rediscovering Hardy's Wessex. The García family have been feeding locals for almost three decades but it was only recently that they completely revamped a simple village eatery to create a stylish and supremely comfortable small hotel-and-restaurant. You arrive by way of a shady terrace, a great place from where to watch the world (and the occasional car or donkey) pass you by. On the two floors above are the bedrooms whose comfort and quality will take you by surprise given their paltry price-tag. Forego a balcony and ask for one that looks out across the prettiest of gardens to the rear of the building. And Casa García's traditional Huelva cuisine is superb. Many ingredients come fresh from the village *huertas* (allotments), the pork and sausages are of the best and the decoration, bright and fresh, is conducive to a memorable, leisurely and satisfying meal.

To see and do: visit to Mezquita in Almonaster, day trips to Portugal, walking in the Natural Park of Aracena.

FINCA LA SILLADILLA

21290 Los Romeros-Jabugo
(Huelva)

Map: 2

Tel: 959 501350 or 658 442071 **Fax:** 959 501351

e-mail: silladi@teleline.es

Web Page: http://es.turinet.net/empresa/lasilladilla

Closed: Never.

Bedrooms: 1 Twin, 1 Suite, 3 Houses with 2 bedrooms and 1 House with 3 bedrooms.

Prices: Twin €64–77 (10700–12840 Ptas), Suite €77–96 (12840–16050 Ptas), 2 bedroomed House €130–154 (21700–25680 Ptas), House for 6 €193–232 (32100–38520 Ptas) including TAX.

Meals: Breakfast included, no Lunch/Dinner available apart from snacks: buy ingredients from farm shop.

Getting there: from Sevilla N-630 north towards Mérida and then the N-433 towards Portugal. Bypass Aracena then Jabugo and just past El Repilado turn left towards Los Romeros and after 3km turn left at sign for La Silladilla.

Management: Beatriz Iglesias Hernández

You may well have heard of Jabugo ham, the mouth-watering delicacy that has always been a favourite present to diplomats visiting Spain, adding a certain weight and sincerity to that farewell handshake at Barajas. You probably won't have heard of Finca La Silladilla, lost as it is in a sea of cistus and oak-forest in a little-known corner of Huelva. You journey here by way of winding country lanes and a narrow stonewalled track which leads you up to the farm – a sight for the sorest of travel-weary eyes. Your room will either be in the main farmhouse or in one of two nearby cottages. The decoration and furnishings are stylish without a hint of showiness, a successful mix of bright fabrics and local base elements such as granite, terracotta and chestnut. Although Silladilla's young live-in staff serve only breakfast (outside in summer, in your room when temperatures fall), there's a bar doubling as a shop/delicatessen where you can buy the makings of a simple, yet gourmet, supper. Wine buffs won't believe their luck when they check the labels on the bottles – and the prices.

To see and do: visit to one of the Jabugo ham *secaderos* (drying shed), walking in the Natural Park of Aracena, day trips to Portugal.

LA POSADA

Calle Médico Emilio González 2
21340 Alájar
(Huelva)

Map: 2

Tel/Fax: 959 125712

e-mail: hotel.laposada@navegalia.com

Closed: Never.

Bedrooms: 3 Twins and 3 Doubles.

Prices: Double/Twin €36 (6000 Ptas) + 7% TAX.

Meals: Breakfast included, Dinner €10 (1600 Ptas) including wine.

Getting there: from Sevilla north on the N-630 towards Mérida and then N-433 towards Portugal to Aracena. Here take N-479 through the town and continue via Linares to Alájar. Take the second sign left into village and the hotel is on the left, just before the square.

Management: Enrique Martín

Alájar is the jewel in the crown of the Aracena park, a tiny village of cobbled streets dominated by the extraordinary Arias Montero peak (climb up late in the afternoon for unforgettable sunset vistas across the park). Just yards from the village's main square, La Posada is a reliable base for forays into the park – by way, perhaps, of the same cobbled paths once trodden by the smugglers whose mules and donkeys sagged beneath heavy loads of Portuguese contraband. At the turn of the century it was known as the Bar de las Estacas, an allusion to the wooden pegs where muleteers would hang their blankets and saddle bags. After a thorough revamp in '96, the place still retains its rustic charm although the bedrooms, in an annex grafted on to the back of the building, are not quite what you might expect   (they are smallish with painted brick walls and simple, modern wooden furniture, functional rather than memorable). But the food is decent (and decently priced, too), Enrique is a cheery host and for travellers on a budget the Posada is a safe bet.

To see and do: visit to the chapel of Nuestra Señora de los Angeles and the abandoned hamlet of Los Madroñeros, day trips to Portugal.

FINCA BUEN VINO

Los Marines   **Map: 2**
21293 Aracena
(Huelva)

Tel: 959 124034   **Fax:** 959 501029

e-mail: buenvino@facilnet.es

Web Page: www.buenvino.com

Closed: July, August, September and Christmas & New Year.

Bedrooms: 4 Doubles.

Prices: Double €168–204 (28000–34000 Ptas) for half-board including TAX.

Meals: Breakfast as well as Dinner for 2 included in price.

Getting there: from Sevilla N-630 north towards Mérida then branch onto the N-433 towards Portugal. Bypass Aracena and village of Los Marines and look for sign for Buen Vino approx 1.5kms after Los Marines on the right (by km95 marker post).

Management: Jeannie & Sam Chesterton

Buen Vino – just writing the words makes me long to return to what must surely be one of Andalucía's most amazing places to stay. This elegant country home (you would never guess that it is only a dozen years old) stands alone in a sea of chestnut and oak forest. It is hard not to feel a frisson of excitement as you approach the house along the long track which cuts an arc up through the estate. And home this is, rather than hotel. A stay with Sam and Jeannie is all about enjoying a ready-made, supremely convivial house-party atmosphere. There isn't the tiniest hint of Forté here. Each bedroom is different to the next, with stacks of paintings, magazines, books and individual decorative flourishes. Downstairs a cosy, panelled dining room provides the perfect stage for Jeannie's cordon bleu suppers. The food is fantastic, wine flows freely and the Chestertons are relaxed and entertaining hosts. The views from the terrace are inspirational. There's a beautiful pool tucked a discrete distance from the house and walks galore straight out from the house. You won't forget the beauty and silence of this deeply rural retreat.

To see and do: visits to the Gruta de las Maravillas cave in Aracena and the villages of the Aracena Natural Park, swimming and picnics at the reservoirs.

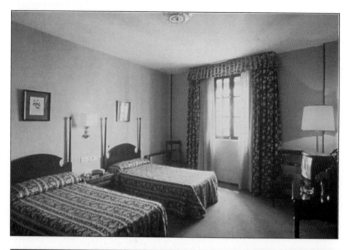

HOTEL SIERRA DE ARACENA

Gran Via 21
21200 Aracena
(Huelva)

Map: 2

Tel: 959 126175 or 959 126019 **Fax:** 959 126218

Closed: Never.

Bedrooms: 8 Singles, 12 Doubles, 8 Twins, 4 Triples, 8 Attic rooms and 2 Suites.

Prices: Single €30 (5000 Ptas), Double/Twin €42 (7000 Ptas), Triple €51 (8500 Ptas), Attic Double/Twin €60 (10000 Ptas), Suite €72 (12000 Ptas) + 7% TAX.

Meals: Breakfast €5 (750 Ptas), no Lunch/Dinner available: several restaurants and tapas bars within walking distance.

Getting there: from Sevilla N-630 north towards Mérida then branch onto the N-433 towards Portugal to Aracena. Hotel is signposed in town centre, close to the main square.

Management: María del Carmen Fernández

Travellers often miss Aracena as they hurry on towards
Portugal or the villages of the Natural Park. Yet this old market
town has a beauty and a timelessness that makes it worth a
long detour. It is also home to the extraordinary Gruta de las
Maravillas cave. The coloured lighting and grande finale of *la
sala de los culos* (look it up) makes the whole experience a
particularly southern-Spanish one. If you plan to spend a night
in town, the Sierra de Aracena should be your hotel. Choose
one of the attic rooms which are worth the extra (3000) pesetas.
Pine-clad with cork-tiled floors, they have a cosier feel than
those on the floors beneath – though these are perfectly
adequate, too. A simple continental breakfast is served in the
quiet guest lounge where a fire will be burning in the colder
months. There is it also a corner bar for a pre- or post-dinner
drink. Right next door is a good restaurant but I would walk just
two minutes to Bar Los Ángeles and order a plate of the
wonderful *lomo* (pork loin). Can pork come better than this?

To see and do: visit to the Gruta de las Maravillas Cave in
Aracena and the Río Tinto mines, walking in the Natural Park of
Aracena.

EL CORTIJO DE LOS MIMBRALES

Ctra del Rocío A-483 km 20   **Map: 2**
21750 Almonte
(Huelva)

Tel: 959 422237 or 670 743991 **Fax:** 959 442443

e-mail: cortijomimbrales@futurnet.es

Web Page: www.cortijomimbrales.com

Closed: Never.

Bedrooms: 6 Doubles, 14 Twins and 6 Cottages sleeping 2, 4 or 6.

Prices: Double/Twin €78–102 (13000–17000 Ptas), Cottage for two €84–168 (14000–28000 Ptas), Cottage for four €99–198 (16500–33000 Ptas), Cottage for six €138–276 (23000–46000 Ptas) + 7% TAX.

Meals: Breakfast €5 (800 Ptas), Lunch/Dinner €14 (2300 Ptas) including wine.

Getting there: from Sevilla west on the A-49 motorway towards Portugal. Exit for Bolullos del Condado and follow A-483 towards Malalascañas. The hotel is on the right, 4km past El Rocío.

Management: José Joaquín Aguirre

Anyone who has journeyed to El Rocío will know that the Doñana Park has a unique beauty, one which somehow eludes capture on film or in prose. Just a five minute drive from the larger-than-life Rocío sanctuary is one of southern Spain's most striking small hotels. The outside of this low, hacienda-style building – it lies at the heart of a vast citrus plantation – is appealing enough but it is the striking use of colour that is so attractive and so original. Everywhere the eye wanders is some striking feature – bright colour washes, exuberant roses, ferns and jasmine, a seductive commingling of antique furnishing and contemporary design. You choose between a room or a cottage: all are four-star comfortable and have been decorated with enormous flair. The night after staying here I made a long journey back to eat a second meal in Los Mimbrales' beautiful, high-ceilinged restaurant. The combination of great food and décor, good-natured, efficient service and the pampering of all five senses make a stay here an unforgettable experience. And there are great beaches nearby, too.

To see and do: Visits to the Doñana National Park, the Sanctuary of the El Rocío Virgin, and the beaches.

HOTEL TORUÑO

Plaza Acebuchal 22
21750 El Rocío
(Huelva)

Map: 2

Tel: 959 442626 or 959 442323 **Fax:** 959 442338

e-mail: HOTELTORUNO@terra.es

Closed: Never.

Bedrooms: 2 Singles, 5 Doubles and 23 Twins.

Prices: Single €40 (6800 Ptas), Double/Twin €57 (9500 Ptas) + 7% TAX.

Meals: Breakfast included, Lunch/Dinner €12 (2000 Ptas) including wine.

Getting there: from Sevilla west on the A-49 motorway towards Portugal then exit for Bolullos del Condado. Then follow A-483 towards Matalascañas to El Rocío. The hotel is 200 yards behind the Rocío Sanctuary.

008

Management: Antonio Pérez Martín

Any estate-agent or hotelier will tell you. Its all about three things – location, location and location. And the location factor comes no higher than at El Toruño. It is just a hundred yards from the shrine of the Rocío Virgin, plum in the centre of the vast Doñana reserve and just yards from the lagoon which brings ornithologists flocking from all over the world. I'll never forget awaking to a blushing dawn and seeing the outline of several dozen flamingos gradually sharpen as a languid February sun burned off the early morning mist. Be sure to get a room with a view. The best, number 225, has windows on two sides and all odd-numbered rooms between 207 and 217 grab a part of that incredible vista. Each bedroom, fittingly, is dedicated to a different species of bird. Even in the bathrooms there are hand-painted pictures of things feathered. You eat in a sister restaurant just across the way where specialities include fish and organic beef raised in the Doñana reserve. A unique village, which out of season feels like a deserted Wild West town, and a unique hotel.

To see and do: visits to the Doñana National Park, the Sanctuary of El Rocío Virgin, and the beaches.

SEVILLA
PROVINCE

Hotels 9 to 20

LAS NAVEZUELAS

A-432 km 43.5, Apartado de Correos 14   **Map: 3**
41370 Cazalla de la Sierra (Sevilla)

Tel: 954 884764 **Fax:** 954 884594

e-mail: navezuela@arrakis.es

Web Page: www.arrakis.es/~navezuela

Closed: 7 January – 20 February.

Bedrooms: 1 Double, 3 Twins, 2 Suites, 4 Apartments for 2 and 1 Apartment for 6.

Prices: Double/Twin €54–57 (9000–9500 Ptas), Suite €66–69 (11000–11500 Ptas), Apartment for two €72-75 (12000–12500) Ptas, Apartment for six €96 (16000 Ptas) or €511 (85000 Ptas) weekly + 7% TAX.

Meals: Breakfast included, Lunch/Dinner €12 (2000 Ptas) excluding wine. In summer only lunches are served, in winter only dinners.

Getting there: from Sevilla follow A-431 to Cantillana. Here take the A-432 via El Pedroso towards Cazalla. Pass the km43 marker post, continue for 500m then turn right and follow a track to Las Navezuelas.

009

Management: Luca Cicorella

Luca and his wife Mariló were already making waves at Las Navezuelas long before the phrase *turismo rural* had entered the vernacular. Thanks to their vision, this small country hotel is now considered a role-model for young folk with similar aspirations. The setting is deeply bucolic – a low, whitewashed *lagar* (a farm where oil was milled) with nothing to interrupt a sweeping panorama of farmland stretching for miles and miles apart from the occasional flock of sheep or goats. The decoration of bedrooms and communal space is fresh, simple and rustic and the overall feel of Las Navezuelas is uncluttered and soothing, the sort of place that could inspire you to put a pen to paper or to reach for the sketch pad. And the food philosophy is similar to the decorative one: traditional and wholesome with no airs of grandeur. Guests return here year after year and so, too, the stork that nests on a rooftop turret. Wake to birdsong, breakfast to Bach, dine to Enya. An aural as well as a visual feast awaits you here and there are wonderful walks straight out from Las Navezuelas.

To see and do: visits to the Huesnar river valley, the Sierra del Viento for panoramic views of the Sierra, and the villages of Cazalla and El Pedroso.

LA CARTUJA DE CAZALLA

Ctra Cazalla - Constantina A455 km 55.2   **Map: 3**
41370 Cazalla de la Sierra
(Sevilla)

Tel: 954 884516   **Fax:** 954 884707

e-mail: cartujsv@teleline.es

Web Page: www.skill.es/cartuja

Closed: 24/25 December.

Bedrooms: 2 Singles, 1 Double, 5 Twins, 4 Suites and 1 House.

Prices: Single €36-54 (6000-9000 Ptas), Double/Twin €60-90 (10000-15000 Ptas), Suite €84-120 (14000-20000 Ptas), House 90-120 (15000-20000 Ptas) + 7% TAX.

Meals: Breakfast included, Lunch €15 (2500 Ptas) including wine, Dinner €21 (3500 Ptas) including wine.

Getting there: From Sevilla follow A-431 to Cantillana and the take take the A-432 via El Pedroso and on to Cazalla. Here follow signs through town for Constantina. After leaving the town on the A-455 continue 2.5km then turn left at sign for La Cartuja.

010

Management: Carmen Ladrón de Guevara

There is nowhere in Spain to stay quite like La Cartuja. It is impossible to imagine what confronted Carmen de Ladrón de Guevara when some two decades back she bought this crumbling Carthusian monastery. She didn't simply hope to restore these old stones, she wanted to breathe new artistic and spiritual life into a building whose remarkable physical setting seems to lift you above the mundane and inspire you to greater things. Hundreds, literally, of lorry-loads of rubble were cleared away and architectural shape and structure gradually re-emerged from the dense foliage that had all but engulfed the building. You stay in one of the monk's cells or perhaps in the annex that Carmen was already hailing as 'a building for the New Millennium' several years back. The silence at night, the extraordinary church and a dinner with Carmen make for a totally unique experience. Thanks to her single-mindedness, La Cartuja has become a forum for artistic debate, a touch-stone for the creative impulse, as well as an extraordinary place to stay.

To see and do: visits to the Huesnar river valley and the Arab and English mines in the Sierra del Hierro, not to mention La Cartuja itself.

HOTEL CORTIJO AGUILA REAL

Ctra Guillena-Burguillos km 4   **Map: 3**
41210 Guillena
(Sevilla)

Tel: 955 785006 **Fax:** 955 784330

e-mail: hotel@aguilareal.com

Closed: Never.

Bedrooms: 10 Twins and 4 Suites.

Prices: Twin €96–114 (16000–19000 Ptas), Suite €132–162 (22000–27000 Ptas) + 7% TAX.

Meals: Breakfast €9 (1500 Ptas), Lunch/Dinner €21 (3500 Ptas) excluding wine.

Getting there: from Sevilla take the N-630 towards Mérida then right on the SE-180 to Guillena. Go through village and at second set of traffic-lights turn right on the SE-181 towards Burguillos. Continue straight across at a roundabout: hotel is signposted to the right after approx. 4km.

011

Management: Isabel Martínez

Several of the grand old *cortijos* (farms) close to Sevilla had a new lease of life breathed into them thanks to a one-off event, the extraordinary 92 Expo, that awakened the world to the narcotic charms of Andalucía. Águila Real is one of their very best, a perfect place to stay if you want to visit Sevilla yet sleep deep in the country, far from the whine of mopeds and buzz of a city that parties on until 5am and later. It is the quintessential Sevillian cortijo, sitting alone on a hill, adrift in a sea of wheat and sunflowers. Massively thick whitewashed walls wrap around a vast courtyard, where dovecot, water trough and stables remind you that this remains a working farm. Inside things are less rustic. There are antiques, bright pastel tones, an honesty bar and a mood of simple elegance. The dining room is particularly intimate and meals include a lot of home-grown produce. You certainly eat very well here. Bedrooms are big with air-conditioning and a serendipitous mix of decorative styles. Choose one leading straight out to the beautiful garden from where you have an amazing view of Sevilla by night.

To see and do: visits to the city of Sevilla, Carmona, and the ruins of Itálica.

CORTIJO TORRE DE LA REINA

Paseo de la Alameda s/n   **Map: 3**
41209 Torre de la Reina (Guillena)
(Sevilla)

Tel: 955 780136 **Fax:** 955 780122

e-mail: info@torredelareina.com

Web Page: www.torredelareina.com

Closed: Never.

Bedrooms: 6 Twins and 6 Suites.

Prices: Twin €96–120 (16000–20000 Ptas), Suite €120–162 (20000–27000 Ptas) + 7% TAX.

Meals: Breakfast €7 (1200 Ptas), Lunch/Dinner €21 (3500 Ptas) excluding wine.

Getting there: from Sevilla take the N-630 north towards Mérida. Shortly after passing the ruins of Itálica turn right towards Córdoba and continue to Algaba. Here at roundabout take C-341 towards Alcalá del Río and after 1.5km turn left to Torre de la Reina. The hotel is on the left as you enter the village.

012

Management: José María Medina Contreras

There is much history wrapped into the fabric of this beautiful old *cortijo* (farm). In the thirteenth century King Ferdinand's army camped here during the conquest of Sevilla. A century later it passed into the possession of Queen María de Molina – thus the name. Recently declared a National Monument, it is now home to one of Andalucía's most seductive small hotels. Here, distilled, is the Romantic vision of Andalucía – layer upon layer of whitewash contrasted by thick bands of ochre, bougainvillaea, geraniums and ferns, air heavy with the scent of jasmine and orange blossom. A number of inter-linked patios lead to a formal garden which is subtly lit at night. You can see why this place is often chosen for wedding parties. The bedrooms and suites (my personal favourite is no. 4) also ooze charm. There are esparto mats, old prints and oil paintings, antique wardrobes and dressers and a full complement of creature comforts. Add to this an authentically andalusian cuisine which looks to the season for its ingredients, a gorgeous vaulted lounge and you begin to get the measure of this remarkable place.

To see and do: the city of Sevilla, Carmona, and the ruins of Itálica.

HOTEL SIMÓN

Calle García de Vinuesa 19
41001 Sevilla
(Sevilla)

Map: 3

Tel: 954 226660 or 954 226615 **Fax:** 954 562241

e-mail: info@hotelsimonsevilla.com

Web Page: www.hotelsimonsevilla.com

Closed: Never.

Bedrooms: 6 Doubles, 18 Twins and 5 Suites.

Prices: Double/Twin €57–78 (9500–13000 Ptas), Suite €78–102 (13000–17000 Ptas) + 7% TAX.

Meals: Breakfast €4 (600 Ptas), no Lunch/Dinner available: huge choice of bars and restaurants close to hotel.

Getting there: along the Avenida de la Constitución passing in front of Cathedral (police will let you pass if you explain that you are heading for hotel) then turn left into Calle Viñuesa. Easier still, park in any city-centre car park (eg El Arenal, Plaza Nueva) and take a taxi to hotel.

013

Management: Francisco Aguayo

The Hotel Simon has long been a favoured sleep-over with travellers to Seville. You couldn't hope to find a better-placed hotel, just yards from the largest Gothic cathedral in Europe, a shake away from the beautiful Calle Sierpes and a stone's throw from the Guadalquivir. Francisco Aguayo has long been at the helm and this gentle-mannered Sevillano (he speaks excellent English) has never been one to rest on his laurels: he is constantly refurbishing and redecorating, determined not only to maintain but also to improve his hotel. A classic facade of wrought-iron rejas and balconies sets the tone of the Simón and this authentically andalusian feel follows through into the columned, ceramic-tiled (18th century) patio-courtyard. Potted ferns and oils, uniformed staff, gilt mirrors and oil paintings all have a slightly out-of-time feel, as does the chandaliered breakfast room. The hotel's bedrooms feel rather less grand but are very comfortable. They vary in style and size, following the original layout of this rambling mansion house. Light sleepers would be best to ask for a room at the rear of the hotel.

To see and do: the Cathedral and the Giralda, the Jewish Quarter, the Plaza de España and the María Luisa Park.

CASA Nº 7

Calle Virgenes 7   **Map: 3**
41004 Sevilla
(Sevilla)

Tel: 954 221581   **Fax:** 954 214527

e-mail: info@casanumero7.com

Web Page: www.casanumero7.com

Closed: Never.

Bedrooms: 4 Doubles and 2 Twins.

Prices: Double/Twin €156 (26000 Ptas) + 7% TAX.

Meals: Breakfast included, no Lunch/Dinner available: huge choice of bars and restaurants close to hotel.

Getting there: park in any city-centre car park (the nearest is 'Cano y Cueto' at the junction of Calle Cano y Cueto and Menéndez Pelayo). Then take a taxi to the hotel.

014

Management: Gonzalo del Río y Gonzalez-Gordon

Recently voted by the London magazine Tatler their Small Hotel of the Year, there is nowhere to stay in the city quite like Casa No.7. A host of details give away a certain nostalgia for the Noel Coward era: scrambled eggs at breakfast, a white-jacketed butler who whisks your suitcase up to your room, an elegant drawing room where you will be served a glass of chilled *fino* (dry sherry) before you head out for dinner. And it will be the very best of finos because Gonzalo, whose family own the González-Byass bodegas, knows more than a thing or two about sherry! Comfort and elegance are the keynotes of the bedrooms he created at Casa No 7. Carefully chosen fabrics, rugs, antique dressers, old prints and oils, family photographs and books give them both a homely and elegant feel, whilst marble floors, double sinks and air-conditioning would delight the most exacting of hotel inspectors. It all feels like a privileged world-within-a-world, of an inner sanctum safe from the heat and the rumble of the Andalusian capital. With luck you may meet Gonzalo and share conversation about changing times in the sherry trade. Like that man Jeeves, he and his hotel are inimitable.

To see and do: the Cathedral and the Giralda, the Jewish Quarter, the Plaza de España and the María Luisa Park.

HOSTERÍA DEL LAUREL

Plaza de los Venerables 5, 41004 Sevilla   **Map: 3**
(Sevilla)

Tel: 954 220295 or 954 210759   **Fax:** 954 210450

e-mail: host-laurel@eintec.es

Web Page: www.hosteriadellaurel.com

Closed: Never.

Bedrooms: 1 Single, 5 Doubles, 21 Twins, 2 Triples and 1 Quadruple.

Prices: Single €30–54 (5000–9000 Ptas), Double/Twin €45–75 (7500–12500 Ptas), Triple €54–90 (9000–15000 Ptas), Quadruple €66–102. (11000–17000 Ptas) + 7% TAX.

Meals: Breakfast €4 (650 Ptas), Lunch/Dinner €27 (4500 Ptas) including wine.

Getting there: the hotel is at a corner of the Plaza de los Venerables close to the Cathedral. Park in any city-centre car park (the nearest is 'Cano y Cueto' at the junction of Calle Cano y Cueto and Menéndez Pelayo) then take a taxi to the hotel. Don´t try to drive here.

015

Management: David Márquez López

The Plaza de los Venerables is right in the middle of Sevilla's Jewish quarter. Wandering its labyrinthine streets remains a beguiling experience even if you are liable to be occasionally engulfed by a group of camera-totting Japanese. And at one corner of this pedestrianised square, the Hostería del Laurel has long been one of my favourite Sevilla hotels. It is one of the city's oldest inns and the place supposedly inspired the writer Zorrilla when he was penning "Don Juan". You enter by way of a rather dark bar-cum-dining room, whose most notable feature is a sea of hams suspended from the ceiling. Further carnage comes in the form of mounted hunting trophies of boar, deer and mountain goats. Beyond is a much lighter, cheerier reception area above which are two floors of bedrooms. Choose one on the second floor to get extra insulation from the restaurant beneath. They are very well-equipped – TVs, phones, air-conditioning – and most of them are of really generous proportions. The Laurel's prices are more than reasonable given the location, and the staff are really helpful, too.

To see and do: the Cathedral and the Giralda, the Jewish Quarter, the Plaza de España and the María Luisa Park.

TABERNA DEL ALABARDERO

Zaragoza 20   **Map: 3**
41001 Sevilla
(Sevilla)

Tel: 954 560637 or 954 502721   **Fax:** 954 563666

e-mail: hotel.alabardero@esh.es

Web Page: www.grupolezama.com

Closed: August.

Bedrooms: 1 Double, 3 Twins and 3 Suites.

Prices: Double/Twin €129 (21400 Ptas), Suite €157 (26100 Ptas) + 7% TAX.

Meals: Breakfast included, Lunch €11 (1800 Ptas) including wine, Dinner €45 (7500 Ptas) including wine.

Getting there: in city centre take Paseo de Colón passing Torre del Oro and immediately in front of the Triana bridge turn right and then take the third right to Alabardero. The hotel has its own car park: staff will park your car for you.

016

Management: Don Luis Lezama Barañano

This elegant Sevilla mansion house was the home of the poet
Cavestany whose most notable literary creation was "A la
sombra de la Giralda" ("Under the Giralda's shadow"). You are,
indeed, just a shake away from Sevilla's most emblematic
architectural feature and very close to the Maestranza bullring.
The hotel was born in 1992 after lengthy and meticulous
restoration work. Its focus is a graceful patio courtyard, a
popular rendezvous for well-heeled sevillanos who meet for
breakfast and for tea and cakes in the afternoon. The restaurant
is amongst the city's best (it won a Michelin star and was a
favourite of the King's mother) and you dine in one of a series
of exquisitely decorated, wonderfully intimate dining rooms.
The culinary philosophy is *cocina de mercado* (whatever is in
season) with a predilection for game: if you go for the lunchtime
menu it won't cost an arm or a leg, either. Bedrooms are regal
affairs, too. They have parquet-floors with excellent linen and
mattresses and a host of details such embroidered bath robes,
hydro-massage baths, a/c and handsome fabrics for bedspreads
and curtains. Well worth a splurge.

To see and do: the Cathedral and the Giralda, the Jewish Quarter,
the Plaza de España and the María Luisa Park.

LAS CASAS DE LA JUDERIA

Callejón Dos Hermanas 7, 41004 Sevilla   **Map: 3**
(Sevilla)

Tel: 954 415150   **Fax:** 954 422170

e-mail: www.juderiazoom.es

Web Page: www.ibernet.net/lascasas

Closed: Never.

Bedrooms: 7 Singles, 97 Doubles/Twins/Junior Suites and 3 Suites.

Prices: Single €67–78 (11000-13000 Ptas), Double/Twin €96–117 (16000–19500 Ptas), Junior Suite €111–132 (18500–22000 Ptas), Suite €168–192 (28000–32000 Ptas) + 7% TAX.

Meals: Breakfast €10 (1600 Ptas), no Lunch/Dinner available: several good restaurants and tapas bars within walking distance.

Getting there: Callejón Dos Hermanas is just off the Calle Esteban, close to the Murillo gardens in the Santa Cruz quarter. Best to park in Cano y Cueto car park at the junction of Calle Cano y Cueto and Menéndez Pelayo and take taxi to hotel (or 2 minute walk from here to the hotel).

017

Management: Miguel Cazorla Cuadro

There are still parts of Sevilla's Santa Cruz where cafés and bars outnumber souvenir shops and where you can get a feel for genuine *sevillano* life. Las Casas de la Judería is just beyond the tourist tract and reached by way of a quiet cul-de-sac. Several town houses once owned by the Duke of Béjar make up this delicious southern fantasy of interconnecting patios, gurgling fountains, ferns, geraniums, orange trees and aspidistra. Every corner of the hotel seems to offer respite from the heat and dust of the city. There are quiet, parquet-floored lounges where old oils, comfy sofas, carefully arranged flowers and stacks of magazines feel like they've been lifted from a Kensington mews. And everywhere you look, some member of the hotel staff is polishing, sweeping, carrying a bag or delivering a gin and tonic. Bedrooms are as elegant as you might expect and surprisingly quiet, and "junior" suites are well worth the extra pesetas. Although larger than most places we include in this book, this hotel remains one of the city's more seductive addresses and has more than a hint of Raffles.

To see and do: the Cathedral and the Giralda, the Jewish Quarter, the Plaza de España and the María Luisa Park.

EL TRIGUERO

Ctra Carmona-El Viso del Alcor km 29   **Map: 3**
41410 Carmona
(Sevilla)

Tel: 955 953626 or 636 844242   **Fax:** 955 953626

Closed: Never.

Bedrooms: 2 Doubles and 7 Twins.

Prices: Double/Twin €48 (8000 Ptas) + 7% TAX.

Meals: Breakfast included, Lunch/Dinner €12 (2000 Ptas) including wine. Advance warning always necessary!

Getting there: from Carmona take the N-392 towards El Viso del Alcor (also signposted for 'Lidl' supermarket). At km29 marker post turn left and follow track to El Triguero.

018

Management: Carmen Vega Salguero

There are still places to stay in Andalucía where simple comfort takes precedence over satellite TV and jacuzzi bath tubs. If you're happy to sleep far from shops, bars and the rumble of traffic, if you don't mind swapping a gleaming hotel reception for a kindly housekeeper whose English is of the "good...please?" variety, if you're happy with simple country cooking rather than burgers and pizza, then this should be your type of place. This alluring *cortijo* (farm) stands alone on a low ridge looking out across mile after mile of farmland, the breadbasket of Sevilla. Seeing the sunset here, feeling the silence of night wrap around the house, is an experience never to be forgotten. El Triguero is far more home than hotel. Here you'll find family portraits and photographs, etchings and the oils, simple yet elegant bedrooms and whirling fans to keep the heat at bay. Do find time for a walk out through the estate by way of the sandy citrus grove that laps up to El Triguero. Try to book the tower room, forgive the rather uninspired offering at breakfast and rejoice in the place's authenticity.

To see and do: visits to Carmona, Sevilla and Osuna.

HOTEL PALACIO MARQUÉS DE LA GOMERA

Calle San Pedro 20
41640 Osuna
(Sevilla)

Map: 4

Tel: 954 812223   **Fax:** 954 810200

e-mail: sanpedro@olanet.net

Web Page: www.hotelpalaciodelmarques.com

Closed: Never.

Bedrooms: 2 Doubles, 16 Twins and 2 Suites.

Prices: Double/Twin €72–90 (12000–15000 Ptas), Suite €120 (20000 Ptas) + 7% TAX.

Meals: Breakfast included, Lunch/Dinner in 'asador' €12 (2000 Ptas) including wine, in main restaurant €24 (4000 Ptas) including wine.

Getting there: from Sevilla take A-92 towards Granada then take first exit for Osuna. At roundabout straight ahead, up Calle Sevilla to Plaza Mayor. Exit at top left of square into Calle Carrera. First left after Calle San Pedro, then second left and left again to hotel.

019

Management: Paco Mulero

One of the great things about living in Andalucía is coming across real gems of towns and villages whose beauty you had never imagined. So it was for me with Osuna, its Calle San Pedro and its remarkable hotel, El Marqués de la Gomera. Nothing quite prepares you for the opulence of its flamboyant portal, its marbled patio and its imposing sweep of baroque staircase. The building's base element is the golden sandstone that is so characteristic of the town's architecture and which adds warmth and substance to the feel of public rooms and bedrooms. The most remarkable of these is the " Torreón" suite from whose lofty perch you have a wonderful roof-scape view of Osuna. All are special, most are cavernous and they are decorated with a successful blend of antiques and contemporary colours and furnishings. Bed linen, mattresses and fabrics are all top-of-the-range. You can choose between two restaurants at Gomera, an informal *asador* (grill) or the more formal Casa del Marqués. It is well worth paying the difference in price in order to enjoy its, and I quote, " elaborate Mediterranean" cuisine.

To see and do: visits to Osuna, Sevilla and Córdoba.

HACIENDA DE SAN RAFAEL

Apartado de Correos 28   **Map: 8**
Carretera Nacional IV (km 594)
41730 Las Cabezas de San Juan
(Sevilla)

Tel: 955 872193 or 020 85632100 (in the UK)
Fax: 955 872201 or 020 85632300 (in the UK)

e-mail: trihotelmktg@dial.pipex.com

Closed: 16 November - 9 March.

Bedrooms: 7 Doubles, 4 Twins and 3 Cottages (Casitas).

Prices: Double/Twin €180 (30000 Ptas), Casita €480 (79865 Ptas) + 7% TAX.

Meals: Breakfast included, Lunch €24 (4000 Ptas), Dinner €42(7000 Ptas) including wine.

Getting there: leave Seville following signs for Cádiz and just before you reach the motorway branch onto the N-IV. Shortly before Las Cabezas de San Juan just past km594 marker post (be sure to keep well to right and indicate!) turn right and follow long drive to San Rafael.

Management: Kuky & Tim Reid

The rolling farmlands stretching south from Sevilla have a unique beauty – a vast, open landscape peppered with whitewashed farmsteads over which high, swaying palms stand sentinel. San Rafael is every inch the classic Andalusian *cortijo* (farm), surrounded by olive groves and with an ochre and white frontage giving onto to an inner courtyard awash with brilliant damask bougainvillaea. Thanks to the decorative razzmatazz and savoir-faire of Tim and Kuky Reid, it is has been transformed into one of Andalucía's most exceptional small hotels. Choose between a *casita* (three share their own pool) or one of the mezzanine rooms. They have masses of space, walk-in bathrooms and their own veranda. They have been decorated with antiques, contemporary furnishings and pieces collected on the Reids many travels to the Far East. Relax with a pre-dinner *fino* (dry sherry) in the most comfortable of lounges (olive oil was once stored here) and choose between eating a sumptuous dinner in the dining room or in the privacy of your terrace. A place to go on any special occasion, and what you will celebrate most is having chosen San Rafael.

To see and do: visits to the Sherry bodegas in Jerez, the city of Sevilla, and the Doñana Park.

CÁDIZ
PROVINCE

Hotels 21 to 39

POSADA DE PALACIO

Calle Caballeros 11
11540 Sanlúcar de Barrameda
(Cádiz)

Map: 8

Tel: 956 364840   **Fax:** 956 365060

Web Page: www.sleepinspain.com

Closed: November – February.

Bedrooms: 4 Doubles, 6 Twins and 4 Suites.

Prices: Double/Twin €48–60 (8000-10000 Ptas), Suite €72 (12000 Ptas) + 7% TAX.

Meals: Breakfast €5 (800 Ptas), Dinner approx €21 (3500 Ptas) including wine.

Getting there: as you arrive in Sanlúcar on A-480 bear right at petrol station. At roundabout continue straight on and at next fork go left into Avenida Doctor Fleming. Pass Barbadillo bodega and Parroquía de la O. Posada is on the left.

021

Management: Renata Strobel

Most visitors to Sanlúcar de Barrameda come to see the enormous bodegas where its dry *manzanilla* wine is produced. There are a host of other reasons for coming here. You can make a boat trip up the Guadalquivir, visit the Doñana Park, wander through the town´s lively covered markets, eat fish fresh off the slab, visit a place which remains unscathed by mass tourism. And to stay at the delightful Posada de Palacio. This rambling mansion seems to encapsulate the mood of the town: sleepy, beguiling and with an air of past glories. An inner patio sets the mood with its ferns, a well, old flags and the classical *alvaro* (bullring sand-coloured) ochre picking out detail on the elegant mouldings. Renata's greeting is relaxed and sincere. She seems to have absorbed the mood of the town. Her rooms vary, following the twists and turns of the building. Some are vast, others smaller, some have sitting rooms or balconies and all are unaffectedly charming. I always look forward to breakfast at the Posada with great coffee, freshly squeezed orange juice and the thought of a day in this wonderful town.

To see and do: visits to the Doñana Park, the Salinas salt beds, the pine forest of Monte Algaida, the old town of Sanlucar and the manzanilla bodegas.

LOS HELECHOS

Plaza de Madre de Dios 9   **Map: 8**
11540 Sanlúcar de Barrameda
(Cádiz)

Tel: 956 361349 or 956 367655   **Fax:** 956 369650

Closed: Never.

Bedrooms: 8 Doubles and 46 Twins.

Prices: Double/Twin €39–54 (6500–9000 Ptas) + 7% TAX.

Meals: Breakfast €3 (500 Ptas), no Lunch/Dinner available:
several good fish bars and restaurants within walking distance.

Getting there: from Jerez take A-480 to Sanlúcar. Here take
Avenida del V° Centenario following signs "Centro Ciudad".
Los Helechos is in the lower part of old town in Calle Baños: if
lost ask for Plazaleta de La Salle.

022

Management: Manuel Reina de los Reyes

Another Sanlúcar hotel which oozes Andalucía from its every corner, Los Helechos is the fruit of the complete renovation of a turn-of-the century mansion. You enter via a massive oak door which leads through to a marble-flagged patio with geometric tiles, wrought-iron grilles, whitewashed walls and masses of potted ferns, from which the hotel takes its name. Just to one side is the reception where you are greeted by a statue of the Rocío Virgin and the friendliest of staff. Bedrooms are reached via a series of patios where lemon trees, potted aspidistra and murmuring fountains strike the same southern note. Most look inwards to the patios. Those giving on to the street are double-glazed to minimise traffic noise. The rooms are medium-sized, simply furnished, sparkling clean and the nicest of them retain their original floor tiles. And you are just a short stroll from the town's delightful palm-fringed square, the Plaza del Cabildo. No visit to the town is complete without a pre-dinner manzanilla and a tapa of *tortilla de camarones* (shrimps deep-fried in batter) at Casa Balbino.

To see and do: visits to The Doñana Park, the Salinas salt beds, the pine forest of Monte Algaida, the old town of Sanlúcar and the manzanilla bodegas.

HOSTAL BAHÍA

Plocia 5　　　　　　　　　　　　　　　　**Map: 8**
11005 Cádiz
(Cádiz)

Tel: 956 259110 or 956 259061　**Fax:** 956 254208

Closed: Never.

Bedrooms: 6 Doubles and 15 Twins.

Prices: Double/Twin €41–51 (6850–8560 Ptas) including TAX.

Meals: No meals available. Several bars and restaurants within walking distance.

Getting there: arriving in Cádiz follow signs for "Casco Antiguo". Park in underground car park of Plaza del Ayuntamiento. Calle Plocia is just off the east side of Plaza.

023

Management: Ramón García

Unless you're feeling flush enough to stay at the Atlántico (too large for this guide), finding a decent place to stay in the old town of Cádiz isn't easy. When researching this guide, I visited a dozen places on the trail of that "perfect small Cadiz" hotel. It just isn't there. However, Hostal Bahía is a good compromise if simple, no-frills comfort is enough for you. This unassuming hostal is just off the Plaza de San Juan Dios, the centre of the old town. Its easy to spot its salmon-coloured facade. The staff are friendly, their English basic. Downstairs is a tiny reception area, beyond which a marble staircase leads to three floors of bedrooms. These are smallish, but not suffocatingly so, with pine furniture and fitted wardrobes. Air-conditioning and satellite tv are unexpected bonuses given the price of the rooms. No breakfast is served but you are just yards from the terrace cafés of the Plaza, a lovely place to start the day with 'tostadas' and coffee. Or walk five minutes to the Plaza de Abastos for *chocolate con churros* (hot chocolate with Andalusian-style donuts)!

To see and do: visits to the old city of Cádiz, the quayside, fortifications and the Alameda gardens, boat trip across the bay to El Puerto de Santa María.

HOTEL CONVENTO DE SAN FRANCISCO

La Plazuela s/n   **Map: 8**
11150 Vejer de la Frontera
(Cádiz)

Tel: 956 451001 or 956 451002   **Fax:** 956 451004

e-mail: convento-san-francisco.tugasa@cadiz.org

Web Page: www.cadiz.org/tugasa

Closed: Never.

Bedrooms: 4 Singles, 4 Twins and 17 Doubles.

Prices: Single €41 (6800 Ptas), Double/Twin €55 (9100 Ptas) + 7% TAX. Add 15% during Holy Week and at Christmas.

Meals: Breakfast €3 (525 Ptas), Lunch/Dinner €13 (2200 Ptas) including wine. Restaurant shut in winter on Tuesdays or Wednesdays.

Getting there: from Cádiz south on the N-340 towards Algeciras. Take the first right turn for Vejer. Go up steep hill and when you reach the town take second turning to your right. Unload bags by hotel and then park.

024

Management: José Manzorro Morillo

Vejer de la Frontera has the unusual credentials of being both hilltop and coastal town, a sort of Ronda by-the-sea. It's always puzzled me why the place doesn't get more visitors: it is a such a beautiful and Andalusian town. The few tourists who pass through tend to stay up in the old town at the Convento de San Francisco, one of a dozen small hotels owned by the regional Cádiz government. The Convent was built in the 17th century, first housing Clarisa nuns before being taken over by the Franciscan order. Nowadays you can leave the hair-shirt at home but you will be sleeping in one of the former cells. These are surprisingly large, have attractive arches of wafer-bricking (the form is mirrored in unusual colour-washed headboards) and the feel is, appropriately, a little Spartan. Downstairs there is no hint of penitence in the menu offered by the Refectorio restaurant: expect to eat well (fish being the obvious choice) and the food, like your room, is remarkably good value. And the lively bar/café is just the place for your post-prandial coffee and brandy.

To see and do: visits to old Vejer and nearby Medina Sidonia, the Atlantic coast, Cape Trafalgar, Tarifa beaches, Playa del Palmar, and day trips to Tangier.

CORTIJO DE LA PLATA

Ctra Atlanterra km 4   **Map: 9**
11393 Zahara de los Atunes
(Cádiz)

Tel: 956 439001   **Fax:** 956 439456

e-mail: cortijoplata@terra.es

Web Page: www.andalucia-riosalado.com/cortijodelaplata

Closed: Early December – middle March.

Bedrooms: 7 Doubles and 8 Twins.

Prices: Double/Twin €60–84 (10000-14000 Ptas) + 7% TAX.

Meals: Breakfast €6 (1000 Ptas), Lunch/Dinner €17 (2750 Ptas) including wine.

Getting there: arriving in Zahara de los Atunes follow signs for the Melía Atlántico for 3km to Urbanización Atlanterra. Here hotel is signposted just to left of the road.

025

Management: José María Castrillón Quintela

Cortijo de la Plata may ring a bell in some ears. This was one of
the very first hotels on the Costa de la Plata, the home of one
Lord Brudenell Bruce who converted the stables of an old army
barracks into a small hotel where he could lodge his many
friends. Later groups of ornithologists came for the spectacle of
annual migrations to and from Africa. More recently (the place
lay empty after B.B.'s death) Chelo and José María Castrillón
have given the building a new lease of life thanks to their flair
for decoration and determination to make every corner of the
place truly special. Furnishings, fittings and fabrics were
chosen with authenticity and comfort in mind, whilst in the
courtyards and gardens hibiscus, vines, palms and cacti were
planted – as well as lawns and an organic vegetable patch. The
views down to the beach, the excellence of the fish and
vegetables (the restaurant is a wonderfully intimate spot), the
decorative charm of the bedrooms and the friendliness of your
hosts help make this one of Andalucía's best small hotels.

To see and do: fine beaches, windsurfing on Tarifa beaches,
golf.

Cádiz Province

100% FUN

Ctra Cádiz - Málaga Km 76
11380 Tarifa
(Cádiz)

Map: 9

Tel: 956 680330   **Fax:** 956 680013

e-mail: 100x100@tnet.es

Web Page: www.tarifanet/100fun

Closed: Early December - middle March.

Bedrooms: 12 Twins, 4 larger Doubles and 6 Suites.

Prices: Twin €48–72 (7900–11900 Ptas), larger Double €58–75 (9800–12500 Ptas), Suite €72–100 (11900–16800 Ptas) including TAX.

Meals: Breakfast included, Lunch/Dinner €21 (3500 Ptas) including wine.

Getting there: from Cádiz take the N-340 towards Algeciras. When you reach the Tarifa Beach 100% Fun is on the left next to La Enseñada, close to the km76 marker post.

026

Management: Ula Walters & Barry Pussell

Any wind surfer knows that the beaches of the Costa de la Luz get the best waves in Europe and it's no accident that the world championships are held right here. Even if you don't surf, the long sweep of the Tarifa beach couldn't fail to move you, with the mountains of the Rif rising a hazy purple above the thumping Atlantic breakers. The road to Cádiz runs between the 100% Fun and the beach but don't let this put you off staying here. Barry and Ula have sculpted the hotel and gardens (and the best surf clothes shop on the coast) so that you immediately forget the tarmac and are instead seduced by the pool, exotic vegetation and the friendly, laid-back feel of the place. The bedrooms and enormous suites are fresh, light and uncluttered with whirling Casablanca-style fans. The tropical-style restaurant (you'll feel more comfortable in shorts and sandals than a suit and tie) looks like its just been lifted from a Bacardi ad. The menu offers welcome respite from steak and chips: good veggie dishes, some spicy Tex-Mex dishes and a few eastern notes as well. The place really does live up to its name.

To see and do: windsurfing on Tarifa beaches, trips to Gibraltar and Morocco, horse-riding along the beach.

HURRICANE HOTEL

Ctra de Málaga a Cádiz   **Map: 9**
11380 Tarifa
(Cádiz)

Tel: 956 684919   **Fax:** 956 680329

e-mail: info@hotelhurricane.com

Web Page: www.hotelhurricane.com

Closed: Never.

Bedrooms: 35 Doubles, Twins and Suites.

Prices: Sea-facing Double/Twin €91–114 (13500-19000 Ptas), Mountain facing Double/Twin €66–90 (11000-15000 Ptas), Family Suite €120–162 (20000-27000 Ptas), Luxury Suite €147–198 (24500–33000 Ptas) + 7% TAX.

Meals: Breakfast included, Lunch €12–15 (2000–2500 Ptas), Dinner €24–30 (4000–5000 Ptas) including wine.

Getting there: from Cádiz take the N-340 south. Hurricane Hotel is to the right of the N-340 approx.7km before you reach Tarifa: signposted.

027

Management: James Whaley

There's nowhere quite like the Hurricane. The hotel owes its existence to James Whaley who saw in a simple roadside "hostal" a vision of better things to come. In the early years most guests were from the windsurfing community but nowadays people come from all over the globe for the pleasure of staying just yards from the mighty breakers of the Atlantic. They also come for the unique feel of the Hurricane which is laid-back, spicy and different. Add to this the fabulous gardens, two pools, a gym, stables, a wind and kite-surfing school and a terrace looking straight out across the waves to the Rif and you begin to get the measure of the place. The best rooms, naturally, are those with sea views but all are stylish in an understated way with a sculptural/decorative debt to things Moroccan (James used to own the Villa Maroc in Essaouira). The Hurricane's food is good, the lunchtime buffet excellent and vegetarians get a great choice of dishes. But be sure to book well in advance because people return year after year.

To see and do: wind-surfing and kite-surfing courses, horse-riding along the beach, day-trips to Morocco by ferry or hydrofoil.

HOTEL LA PEÑA

Ctra N340 km 78.4   **Map: 9**
11380 Tarifa
(Cádiz)

Tel: 956 681070   **Fax:** 956 681070

Closed: November – Easter

Bedrooms: 4 Doubles and 14 Twins.

Prices: Double/Twin €51–67 (8500–11200 Ptas) + 7% TAX.

Meals: Breakfast €2 (450 Ptas), no Lunch/Dinner available: good food at Hurricane just across the road.

Getting there: from Tarifa take N-340 towards Cádiz. Hotel La Peña is at km78.4, to the right of the N-340 shortly before you reach the Hurricane.

028

Management: Antonio del Castillo

If you are headed for the Tarifa beaches and can bear to stay just back from the sea, then this friendly small hotel is a brilliant venue. You cut up and away from the busy N-340 along an oleander-lined drive to a low, cherry-coloured building. Its well-tended lawns, the surrounding greenery and its single storey is rather reminiscent of the bungalow-style hotels of India. The Castrillo family take huge care of La Peña. The day I visited, paint was being retouched, lawns mown and floors polished, yet they still gave me plenty of their time. Their bedrooms either give on to a quiet patio to the rear of the bar/reception (numbers 10-18) or are in an annex just back from the pool (numbers 1-9), from where there are views of Morocco. All are large, spotless, with firm mattresses, large fitted wardrobes and are painted in a fresh, lemony colour – so never mind those sugary prints. Although only breakfast and drinks are served in the small, plant-filled restaurant-cum-reception, you can walk to the Hurricane for dinner or head into Tarifa for good eats.

To see and do: Tarifa beaches, windsurfing, whale-watching etc., Roman ruins of Baelo Claudio at Bolonia, day trip to Morocco by ferry or hydrofoil.

SANCHO IV

Calle Sancho IV el Bravo 18　　　　　　　　　　**Map: 9**
11380 Tarifa
(Cádiz)

Tel: 956 627083　**Fax:** 956 627055

e-mail: hotelsancho4@terra.com

Web Page: www.enjoytarifa.com

Closed: Never.

Bedrooms: 1 Single, 4 Doubles and 7 Twins.

Prices: Single €30–60 (5000-10000 Ptas), Double/Twin €48–84 (8000–14000 Ptas) + 7% TAX.

Meals: Breakfast €5 (750 Ptas), Lunch/Dinner €21 (3500 Ptas) including wine.

Getting there: arriving in Tarifa follow signs for El Casco Antiguo. The hotel is at the very heart of the old town next to the church of San Mateo: you pass it as you follow the one-way system through the town.

029

Management: Julio Giner Montoro

Twenty years ago, few foreigners visited Tarifa, discouraged by the *levante* (a wind from the East) that blows hard across the town for so much of the year. Ironically that same wind has brought the town prosperity. It has become the windsurfing capital of Europe as well as a hip night-time destination for the youth of Algeciras. Many head for the beautiful café of Sancho IV, a venue for good flamenco, jazz and other musical happenings. The place reminded me of a huge French bistro but its amazing tiled-mosaic floor, Moroccan chairs and tables and cherry-coloured walls contrasted against natural stone give it a much more exotic, designerish feel. The bedrooms (light sleepers should ask for one on the top floor) have the same spicy ingredients: more Moroccan furniture, interesting colours and contemporary paintings. Be sure to have lunch or dinner here: a few good dishes rather than several mediocre ones is the food philosophy. The *atún encebollado* I tried was wonderful and when I asked the waiter to recommend a wine, he whisked out the very last bottle of his favourite, irreplaceable Ribera. Now there's service for you.

To see and do: day trips from here to Morocco by ferry or hydrofoil, the Tarifa beaches, windsurfing .

CASA CONVENTO LA ALMORAIMA

Ctra Algeciras-Ronda **Map: 10**
11350 Castellar de la Frontera
(Cádiz)

Tel: 956 693002   **Fax**: 956 693214

Closed: Never.

Bedrooms: 3 Singles, 1 Double and 13 Twins.

Prices: Single €56 (9300 Ptas), Twin €69 (11500 Ptas), Double €90 (15000 Ptas) including TAX.

Meals: Breakfast €6 (1000 Ptas), Lunch/Dinner €20 (3250 Ptas) including wine.

Getting there: from Algeciras take the N-340 towards Málaga then branch onto C-3331 towards Jimena de la Frontera. La Almoraima is signposted to the left close to the turning for Castellar de la Frontera.

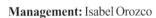

030

Management: Isabel Orozco

Almoraima has a colourful history. It was built as a convent by the Countess of Castellar in 1603 and later snatched by the Duke of Medinacelli and became a hunting lodge. Sacked by Napoleon's troops, it was then expropriated by the state and given back to the Medinacelli family only to be sold to a bank, which went bust. Finally it was once again expropriated and turned into one of Andalucía's most seductive hotels. Although Almoraima's balustraded facade and Florentine belfry are a rather grand entrée, once you enter its cloistered patio you are enveloped in a magical and intimate world-within-a-world, where plants, birdsong and the scent of orange blossom are conducive to blissful relaxation. The bedrooms are sober and comfortable, there's an elegant lounge with an honesty bar and authentic Andalusian cuisine served in a chandaliered dining room by the hotel's willing staff. Should you stay here you won't want for space: you are surrounded by 16000 hectares of estate which is yours to explore on foot or on horseback. And be sure to visit nearby Castellar de la Frontera.

To see and do: visits to Castellar de la Fontera and the Natural Park of Los Alcornocales, day trips to Gibraltar and Morocco.

EL CONVENTO

Calle Maldonado 2
11630 Arcos de la Frontera
(Cádiz)

Map: 9

Tel: 956 702333   **Fax:** 956 704128

e-mail: elconvento@viautil.com

Web Page: www.webdearcos.com/elconvento

Closed: Never.

Bedrooms: 1 Single, 3 Doubles and 3 Twins with own terrace, 2 Doubles and 2 Twins without terrace.

Prices: Single €30–48 (5000-8000 Ptas), Double/Twin with terrace €54–72 (9000-12000 Ptas), Double/Twin without terrace €42–60 (7000-10000 Ptas) + 7% TAX.

Meals: Breakfast €5 (800 Ptas), Lunch €24 (4000 Ptas) including wine, Dinner €30 (5000 Ptas) excluding wine.

Getting there: arriving in Arcos follow signs up to the Parador: its narrow but unless you have a wide vehicle it can be done! Park in the square in front of Parador. Walk to end of Calle Escribano (narrow street to the left of the Parador), turn right and Hotel El Convento is on the right.

031

Management: María Moreno Moreno

El Convento nudges right up to the edge of Arcos' spectacular cliff and the views have to be seen to be believed. Where else can you look down on a kestrel in full flight? It was once part of the adjacent Convent of the Sisters of Mercy, but Fate is a strange thing. The hotel's owner was a postman and when delivering the Sister's post he was amazed to see a large part of the edifice lying empty. The rest is hotel history and after years of constant improvements María and husband José have created a small, friendly, intimate and utterly Andalusian hotel. They recently completely revamped the breakfast room/bar area with bright geometric wall tiles and attractive rush-seated chairs: this is now a lovely space in which to start the day (or end it with a night cap from the bar). Book a room that faces cliff wards and be sure to eat at the hotel's sister restaurant which is just 50 yards along the street and also called El Convento. It's one of the best in the province of Cádiz, as testified to by numerous gastronomic prizes which are displayed as you enter the restaurant.

To see and do: the old town of Arcos, guided visit to the Roman site in nearby Sierra Aznar, bodegas and Royal Ecuestrian School in Jerez.

HOTEL LOS OLIVOS DEL CONVENTO

Paseo de Boliches, 30   **Map: 9**
11630 Arcos de la Frontera
(Cádiz)

Tel: 956 700811   **Fax:** 956 702018

e-mail: mmoreno0237@viautil.com

Web Page: http://losolivos.profesionales.org

Closed: Never.

Bedrooms: 2 Singles, 4 Doubles and 13 Twins.

Prices: Single €30–36 (5000-6000 Ptas), Double/Twin €48–60 (8000-10000 Ptas) including TAX.

Meals: Breakfast €6 (900 Ptas), no Lunch/Dinner available but good food in sister restaurant El Convento: Lunch €24 (4000 Ptas) including wine, Dinner €30 (5000 Ptas) excluding wine.

Getting there: arriving in Arcos follow signs for the Parador. As you follow the one-way system up into the old part of town you'll see the hotel just to the left of the road.

032

Management: José Roldán Caro

José Roldán Caro is, as the Spanish would say, *un fenómeno*. Owner of another Arcos hotel and the town's best restaurant, organiser of gastronomic and cultural events promoting his beloved Arcos, he still somehow manages to find time to manage Los Olivos and attend to diners in person at his restaurant. And with considerable grace, to boot. Los Olivos, his second hotel, is as Andalusian as the man himself. You pass it as you climb up into the old town centre: a brilliant white, terracotta-tiled facade with arched balcony and beautiful wrought-iron *rejas* (wrought-iron window/door grilles). No surprise that the Andalusian flag (along with the Spanish one) hangs above the door. The hotel's focal point is a plant-filled patio surrounded by a covered gallery with comfortable cane sofas and arm chairs: there are masses of plants. A wide sweep of staircase leads to the sparkling bedrooms, some looking out to the valley beneath Arcos, others facing the inner patio (light sleepers would prefer one of these). Los Olivos' staff are incredibly friendly and its prices are, too.

To see and do: the old town of Arcos, the bodegas & Royal Ecuestrian School in Jerez, the Grazalema Natural Park and the white villages.

LA CASA GRANDE

Calle Maldonado 10 **Map: 9**
11630 Arcos de la Frontera
(Cádiz)

Tel: 956 703930   **Fax:** 956 703930

e-mail: lacasagrande@lacasagrande.net

Web Page: www.lacasagrande.net

Closed: 15 December – 27 December.

Bedrooms: 2 Twins and 2 Suites.

Prices: Twin €66 (11000 Ptas), Suite €78–84 (13000-14000 Ptas) + 7% TAX.

Meals: Breakfast €5 (900 Ptas), tapas-style lunches and suppers €12 (2000 Ptas) including wine.

Getting there: follow signs up to the Parador: its narrow but unless you have a wide vehicle it can be done! Park in the square in front of Parador. Walk to end of Calle Escribano (narrow street to the left of the Parador), turn right, pass Hotel El Convento and then turn left. La Casa Grande is on the right.

033

Management: Elena Posa

There is, of course, an art to good living and the Spanish are perhaps the Europeans who live the Epicurean ideal to the fullest. A stay at La Casa Grande as guest of this immensely attractive and intelligent Catalan couple is certainly about the better things in life. The position is incredible: this 273 year-old house nudges right up to the very edge of the Arcos cliff. It is a classic seigneurial town house with a grand portal, columned inner patio, huge reception rooms, three floors high. Elena and Ferrán have given the house new life by creating four guest bedrooms/suites in its upper floors and decorating them with considerable panache, happily mixing the original traditional Andalusian features (there are wonderful original floors) with contemporary colours and Ikea-ish furnishings. La Casa Grande's breakfast is a feast of orange juice, cheese, wonderful bread and a *degustación* (a tasting) of different olive oils. But what you will most remember is its rooftop terrace where Elena will serve you a light, *tapas* supper. The views from here are simply beyond belief.

To see and do: the old town of Arcos, the bodegas and Royal Ecuestrian School in Jerez, the white villages, and the towns of El Bosque, Benamahoma and Prado del Rey.

CORTIJO BARRANCO

Apartado de Correos 169   **Map: 9**
11630 Arcos de la Frontera
(Cádiz)

Tel: 956 231402   **Fax:** 956 231209

e-mail: fincabarranco@jazzfree.com

Web Page: www.cortijobarranco.com

Closed: 20 December – 2 January.

Bedrooms: 7 Doubles, 6 Twins and 1 Apartment.

Prices: Double/Twin €72 (12000 Ptas), Apartment €120 (20000 Ptas) including TAX.

Meals: Breakfast included, Dinner €15 (2500 Ptas) including wine, weekdays only.

Getting there: From Arcos de la Frontera take the A-372 towards El Bosque. After 5.7km, at end of long straight section, turn left at the sign for Barranco then follow a track for 2km to the farm.

034

Management: María José Gil Amián

Barranco, of all the *cortijo* (farm) hotels of Andalusia, is perhaps the one that gives you the best feeling for how life on one of these vast country estates is lived. Cutting in from the Arcos road you follow three kilometers of track upwards, then round a final bend to the farm, adrift in a landscape of olives and wheat fields. Massive walls defy the Andalusian sun and crenelated towers remind you that this was once *frontera* (frontier) country - even if the Moors had long since left Spain when an olive mill was built in 1752. The farm wraps round a classic, arched inner courtyard where you are greeted by the Gil Amián family or Barranco's resident housekeepers before being shown to your room. The leitmotif here is unaffected, old-fashioned comfort: good linen, antique bedsteads with thick mattresses, bright kilims contrasted against the traditional whitewashed walls. There is a comfortable lounge with billiards table and honesty bar and breakfasts and dinners are wholesome affairs, served in the beautiful high-ceilinged dining room. A caring gesture is the provision of electric blankets in winter. Quiet, remote and enchanting.

To see and do: Arcos de la Frontera & Medina Sidonia, the Grazalema Natural Park, the bodegas & Royal Ecuestrian School in Jerez.

HACIENDA BUENA SUERTE

Apartado de Correos 60   **Map: 9**
11650 Villamartín
(Cádiz)

Tel: 956 231286   **Fax:** 956 231275

e-mail: hacienda@dysli.net

Web Page: www.dysli.net

Closed: Never.

Bedrooms: 2 Singles, 2 Doubles and 9 Twins.

Prices: Single €42 (7000 Ptas), Double/Twin €72 (12000 Ptas).

Meals: Breakfast included, Lunch €15–18 (2500-3000 Ptas) including wine.

Getting there: From Ronda take the C-339 towards Sevilla. then the N-342 towards Jerez. 7km before Villamartín turn left for El Bosque/Ubrique. The large white entrance gate to the Hacienda is on the left, 1.5km after you turn off the N-342.

035

Management: Magda & Jean-Claude Dysli

In the last foothills of the Grazalema mountains, surrounded by a vast estate of olive groves and indigenous oak forest, Hacienda Buena Suerte would be a great choice for anyone with an interest in horses. Jean-Claude Dysli gives lessons in Western-style riding: he is one of the world's best instructors, dividing his time between the USA, Spain and his native Switzerland. You won't see finer quarter horses in Europe and even as an equine ignoramus I found it fascinating to watch his pupils being put through their paces (most come from Germany). The stables are just across from the main *cortijo* (farm) which is graced by high palm trees and rampant bougainvillaea. In the bedrooms the emphasis is on uncluttered comfort with prints of horses and animal skins giving them a rather Wild West, frontier-country feel. Life at Buena Suerte centres round a huge beamed dining-room/bar where lunches and dinners are eaten around big bench tables: much of what you eat is farm-raised and organically grown. Non-riders would enjoy this place, too, and there are beautiful walks out through the estate.

To see and do: riding with Jean-Claude and Magda, visits to the Grazalema Natural Park, Ronda, Sevilla and Jerez.

HOSTAL CASA DE LAS PIEDRAS

Calle las Piedras 32
11610 Grazalema
(Cádiz)

Map: 10

Tel: 956 132014 or 956 132323 **Fax:** 956 132014

Closed: Never.

Bedrooms: 2 Doubles and 14 Twins (all en suite) and 16 rooms which share bathrooms and toilets.

Prices: Double/Twin €33 (5500 Ptas), Double/Twin sharing €18 (3000 Ptas) including TAX.

Meals: Breakfast €3 (500 Ptas), Lunch/Dinner €8 (1300 Ptas) including wine.

Getting there: From Ronda take the C-339 towards Sevilla. Pass Venta La Vega and shortly afterwards turn left to Grazalema. Here in the main square turn sharp right and head up the street to the left of the Unicaja bank. Casa de las Piedras is on the right after about 150m.

036

Management: Rafael & Katy Lirio Sánchez

It's a dozen years since I first stayed at Las Piedras and this little hostal seems to get better and better as the years go by. It's long been popular with walking groups from the UK who base themselves here in the sure knowledge that a comfortable bed, good country cooking and a friendly welcome are guaranteed. The hostal is just up from the main square, its whitewashed facade with old wrought-iron window grilles and two fine portals giving it a rather grand look. You'll be greeted with a smile by Katy and Rafael, who also works as a taxi driver and can run you to the starting point of local walks. The best bedrooms are in the new wing of Las Piedras. Try to book one on the top floor. These are quieter and two of them manage to grab a view out across the village's terracotta rooftops. The rooms in the older part of Las Piedras are much more basic and share bathrooms and toilets (although the plan is to renovate this part in the coming year). In spite of the growing numbers of visitors, and the coach parties which arrive at the weekend, Grazalema is well worth a detour and the walking here is magnificent.

To see and do: walking in Grazalema Park, a visit to the Blanket Factory in the village centre, and visits to other white villages.

HOTEL PUERTA DE LA VILLA

Plaza Pequeña 8   **Map: 10**
11610 Grazalema
(Cádiz)

Tel: 956 132376 or 956 132405   **Fax:** 956 132087

e-mail: info@grazhotel.com

Web Page: www.grazhotel.com

Closed: Never.

Bedrooms: 3 Doubles, 23 Twins, 2 Suites and 5 Apartments.

Prices: Double/Twin €79–99 (13200-16500 Ptas), Suite €153–192 (25600-32000 Ptas), Apartments (according to number of occupants) €79–186 (13200-31000 Ptas) + 7% TAX.

Meals: Breakfast €9 (1400 Ptas), Lunch/Dinner €18 (2975 Ptas) including wine.

Getting there: From Ronda take the C-339 towards Sevilla. Pass Venta La Vega and shortly afterwards turn left to Grazalema. As you arrive in the village the hotel is on the left, just before a church and the main square.

037

Management: Rodrigo Valle Naranjo

Hotel Puerta de la Villa, as the name implies, is next to the old entrance to Grazalema. In the past you reached it after a stiff climb via the old Roman road that zigzags up from the river valley. This was the first four star hotel to be opened in the Sierra, a sign of changing times in the mountains of Cádiz. The facade of the building is in synch with traditional white-village architecture but once through the heavy old wooden door, things take on a different note. Uniformed staff greet you in the large reception area from where a marble staircase (or lift) leads up to carpeted corridors and the bedrooms. These stylishly marry Ronda-style rustic furniture with subtle colour washes and have a full complement of gadgetry – air-conditioning, satellite TVs, phones in the bathroom. The best (numbers 8-12 and 22-26) have views out across the valley. The restaurant shares the view and the food is good, the chef having been headhunted from one of the Province's best-known eateries. And if you are tempted to over indulge, a sauna and a gym await you in the basement.

To see and do: walking in the Grazalema Natural Park, a visit to the Blanket Factory in the village centre, and visits to other nearby white villages.

HOSTAL EL ANÓN

Calle Consuelo 36
11330 Jimena de la Frontera
(Cádiz)

Map: 10

Tel: 956 640113 **Fax:** 956 641110

e-mail: elanon@viautil.com

Web Page: www.andalucia.com/jimena/hostalanon

Closed: 19 June - 19 July.

Bedrooms: 2 Singles, 5 Twins, 5 Doubles and 1 Apartment.

Prices: Single €27–29 (4500–4750 Ptas), Double/Twin €47–49 (7800–8200 Ptas), Apartment €54–58 (9000–9700 Ptas) including TAX.

Meals: Breakfast €3 (400 Ptas), Lunch/Dinner €18 (3000 Ptas) including wine. Bar snacks also available. Restaurant & bar closed on Wednesdays.

Getting there: From Málaga take the N-340 west towards Algeciras and at the roundabout in Pueblo Nuevo de Guadiaro turn right to San Martín del Tesorillo. Here take CA-513 west and then turn right onto the A-369 to Jimena. El Anon is in the village centre, signposted to the left.

038

Management: Suzanna Odell

Suzanna Odell (Susie to her many friends) has lived in Jimena for many years and opened El Anon long before the hilltop villages of this part of Spain became known by the ex-pat community. A number of village houses were gradually wrapped into the fabric of the *hostal* (a simple inn), creating an intimate, organic and delightfully rambling place to stay. Each bedroom is different to the next. Some give onto inner patio-courtyards, others to the village's whitewashed streets, making some of them light, others rather darker. The emphasis is on simple, rustic, uncluttered comfort rather than on gadgetry and four-star finery. You can see why El Anon's rooms appeal to walkers and the place has long been popular with groups from the UK who use it as a base from which to explore the paths through the Alcornocales Natural Park. The restaurant and bar feel as cosy as the rest of the hotel and Susie's cuisine looks mostly to Spain and Morocco for its inspiration. The staff are young and friendly and the whole place is imbued by Susie's relaxed and friendly nature.

To see and do: a visit to Castellar de la Frontera, wonderful walks along the Hozgarganta river valley, and day trips to Gibraltar and Morocco.

POSADA LA CASA GRANDE

Calle Fuentenueva 42
11330 Jimena de la Frontera
(Cádiz)

Map: 10

Tel: 956 640578   **Fax:** 956 640491

e-mail: tcag@mx4.retemail.es

Web Page: www.posadalacasagrande.com

Closed: Never.

Bedrooms: 3 Doubles and 2 Twins sharing 3 baths & wcs and 3 Suites with en suite bathrooms.

Prices: Double/Twin €30–36 (5000–6000 Ptas), Suite €48–60 (8000–10000 Ptas) including TAX.

Meals: Breakfast €5 (750 Ptas), no Lunch/Dinner available but great tapas in bar next door!

Getting there: From Málaga take the N-340 west towards Cádiz. At the roundabout in Pueblo Nuevo de Guadiaro turn right to San Martín del Tesorillo. Here take CA-513 west and then turn right onto the A-369 to Jimena. Here follow main street through village and take the last right down hill to La Casa Grande.

039

Management: Mercedes & Tom Andrésen

The name Andrésen doesn't sound exactly Spanish, its true. But Tom and Mercedes both grew up in Jimena, went to the same school and years later met again....and married. They are young, multilingual and exceptionally friendly, and seem ideally suited to their newly-adopted profession as innkeepers. La Casa Grande is in fact three village houses and an old stable block which have been linked together to create an organic, interesting and supremely welcoming inn. The atmosphere is far more that of home than hotel. There is a beautiful lounge up beneath the eaves with masses of books, plants and a view over the village rooftops: Paco the pet iguana and a purring cat should be around to greet you. Downstairs is another lounge, a bar area and more plants and books. Rugs add warmth and colour to the traditional tile floors, a hammock awaits you at siesta time. La Casa Grande's bedrooms vary in size and configuration mixing antique with modern furniture and they have bright bedspreads and simple bathrooms. Only breakfast is served but there is a fantastic *tapas* bar.

To see and do: bird-watching and walking in the Natural Park of Los Alcornocales, the Tarifa beaches, and day trips to Morocco by boat or hydro-foil.

MÁLAGA
PROVINCE

Hotels 40 to 77

EL PAPUDO

11340 San Martín del Tesorillo
(Málaga)

Map: 10

Tel: 95 2854018   **Fax:** 95 2854018

e-mail: papudo@mercuryin.es

Web Page: www.andalucia.com

Closed: Never.

Bedrooms: 3 Doubles and 8 Twins.

Prices: Double/Twin €63 (10500 Ptas) including TAX.

Meals: Breakfast included, no Lunch/Dinner available: simple restaurants in village just a short drive from farm.

Getting there: from Málaga take the N-340 west towards Cádiz. At roundabout in Pueblo Nuevo de Guadiaro turn right to San Martín del Tesorillo. As you arrive in San Martín road bends hard left: here take dirt track straight ahead (signposted 'Viveros Papudo'). House is signposted to the left after 1.5km.

040

Management: Vivien & Michael Harvey

The small village of San Martín lies at the southern end of the Guadiaro valley, just a few miles inland from Sotogrande. The exceptionally mild, moist climate of this part of Andalucía means that subtropical species thrive and the village is surrounded by vast plantations of fruit trees. This fecund climate also explains the existence of a number of garden centres. The Harveys own one of the best of them and they recently restored and renovated the neighbouring *cortijo* (farm) to create a small country B&B. The gardens, as you'd expect, are fantastic and anyone with even a passing interest in things horticultural will love the symphony of colour and texture that Vivien and Michael have created from plants, trees and shrubs. When converting the old granary to create the bedrooms, they tried to change as little as possible. Lots of the original beams and tiles are still in place and the abundance of wood gives the rooms a warm and welcoming feel. This could be a great choice if you're looking for a quiet place to really unwind and there are good restaurants within a short drive.

To see and do: a visit to Castellar de la Frontera, dolphin watching out from La Linea, the beaches next to the marina in Sotogrande.

CORTIJO LA VIZCARONDA

Lista de Correos
29692 Sabanillas
(Málaga)

Map: 10

Tel: 95 2113742   **Fax:** 95 2113742

e-mail: info@vizcaronda.com

Web Page: www.vizcaronda.com

Closed: Never.

Bedrooms: 2 Doubles and 2 Twins.

Prices: Double/Twin €90–120 (15000–20000 Ptas) including TAX.

Meals: Breakfast included, no Lunch/Dinner available: loads of restaurants in Sabanillas and Manilva.

Getting there: from Estepona take N-340 towards Algeciras. In Sabanillas turn right at Campsa petrol station towards Manilva. Just past 2km post turn hard left and then right after just 50 yards. Go down a narrow road into valley, pass stands of bamboo then follow a concrete track up to Vizcaronda.

041

Management: John Waddingham & Henry Were

John and Henry looked at virtually every property that was for sale along this part of southern Spain's coastal fringe before being shown the crumbling walls of an old wine bodega, high on a hill close to Manilva. They were hooked and who wouldn't have been when faced with that view down to the Mediterranean and across to the Moroccan Rif? Five years on, they have created a real home-away-from home, a wonderfully intimate hotel that manages to match its setting. Vizcaronda has been decorated with buckets of razzmatazz: there are rich colours, snazzy fabrics, lamps and tables from the Far East and stacks of antiques that once graced the coaching inn they left behind in England. The four bedrooms, reached by way of a long wafer-bricked corridor, also have a festive, almost theatrical feel: splendid fabrics, baldequin beds, arches, old prints and curios and each with its own private terrace. Although John and Henry only prepare breakfasts, they join guests for drinks and canapés before dinner (there are masses of restaurants nearby). A hugely convivial house-party atmosphere awaits you at Vizcaronda.

To see and do: a visit to Castellar de la Frontera, day trips to Morocco and Gibraltar, beaches and watersports.

EL NOBO

Apartado de Correos 46　　　　　　　　　**Map: 10**
29480 Gaucín
(Málaga)

Tel: 95 2151303　**Fax:** 95 2117207

e-mail: info@elnobo.co.uk

Web Page: www.elnobo.co.uk

Closed: 20 December – 3 January & July and August.

Bedrooms: 1 Double, 1 Twin and 1 Cottage.

Prices: Double/Twin €108 (18000 Ptas), Cottage (minimum stay 3 nights) €108 (18000 Ptas) including TAX.

Meals: Breakfast included, Dinner €27 (4500 Ptas) including wine.

Getting there: from Estepona N-340 towards Cádiz then right via Manilva to Gaucín. Here right opposite petrol station into village to small square by a *farmacía* (on your right). Here turn the car round and follow a narrow road down past La Fructuosa restaurant. El Nobo to the left of the track 1km down this road.

042

Management: Sally Von Meister

You'll need to travel a very long way to find as magnificent a setting as this. El Nobo straddles a hilltop just beneath Gaucín with views that defy description. Be here at sunset and you'll understand why this is one of the most photographed houses in Andalucía. Tuffy von Meister told me that the most common reaction of new-arrivals when faced with the view down to Gibraltar and to the mountains of North Africa is simply an awe-inspired "wow!". The interior design and décor gets all of the journalists purring: Condé Nast, the Sunday Times, Casa y Campo have all waxed lyrical about the country-style furnishings, beautiful colour washes and the stunning garden that has been sculpted amongst the natural rock. And foodies will love staying at El Nobo: you'll want for nothing at breakfast and Sally's dinners are legendary. She describes her cooking as "very Mediterranean". There is often fish and her choice of vegetables and fruit follows the seasons. The accompanying wines, chosen by Tuffy, are excellent. And there are fantastic walks straight out from the house.

To see and do: walking in the Gaucín area, visits to Ronda and the white villages, day trip to Tangier.

HOTEL CASABLANCA

Calle Teodoro de Molina 12
29480 Gaucín
(Málaga)

Map: 10

Tel: 95 2151019   **Fax:** 95 2151019

Closed: End October - early March.

Bedrooms: 4 Doubles, 1 Twin and 2 Family rooms.

Prices: Double/Twin €60–84 (10000–14000 Ptas), Family room €72–84 (12000–14000 Ptas) including TAX.

Meals: Breakfast included, Lunch €18–21 (3000–3500 Ptas) including wine/Dinner €24–27 (4000–4500 Ptas) including wine. Restaurant closed on Mondays.

Getting there: from Estepona take the N-340 towards Cádiz then right via Manilva to Gaucín. Here right opposite petrol station into village to small square by a 'farmacía' (it will be on your right). Here hotel is signposted: park anywhere round here then ask any local the way to Casablanca!

043

Management: Susan & Mike Dring

The naming of this hotel was inspired. This is, indeed, a white village house, a genuine *casa blanca*. And from here there are incredible views of Morocco, even if you can't quite see as far as the town that Bogart and Bergman made famous. This enormous village house started life as a bodega, then later was given a much grander air when it became the home of a Spanish *marquesa*. She shipped in an amazing bannistered staircase, raised ceilings, added stucco mouldings and parquet floors and brought mirrors (still in place today) all the way from Venice. You enter via a light and airy dining room where a Belgian chef has earned a reputation amongst the local ex-pats for excellent, imaginative cuisine: try his magret of duck in cherry sauce, gratin of tiger prawns or chocolate pudding. There is a covered patio where you eat during the warmer months which looks out across a second patio and pool. Most bedrooms are wrapped round these patios and two of them grab that amazing view south. But if you plan to stay at Casablanca be sure to book early. Mike and Sue's hotel is deservedly hugely popular.

To see and do: walking in the Gaucín area, day trip to Tangier, visits to Ronda and the white villages.

LA FRUCTUOSA

Calle Luis de Armiñan 67   **Map: 10**
29480 Gaucín
(Málaga)

Tel: 95 2151072 or 617 692784 **Fax:** 95 2151580

e-mail: lafructuosa@eresmas.com

Closed: Never.

Bedrooms: 3 Doubles and 2 Twins.

Prices: Double/Twin €75 (12500 Ptas) including TAX.

Meals: Breakfast included, Lunch/Dinner €21 (3500 Ptas) including wine. Restaurant closed on Thurdays in summer and for whole of November.

Getting there: from Estepona take the N-340 towards Cádiz then right via Manilva to Gaucín. Here turn right at the first junction and follow this street into the village to a small square by a 'farmacía' (it will be on your right). Here turn the car round and follow a narrow road down the hill to La Fructuosa.

044

Management: Luis & Jesús

Ask any of Guacín's ex-pat community where best to eat in the village and they invariably answer "La Fructuosa". Its cuisine looks to the Med' for inspiration and to whatever is in season for its ingredients. You might be served dolmas, tapenade or hummus as an apéritif, followed by an excellent *ibérico* (Iberian) sirloin steak or a kebab with Moroccan style spices. Luis and Jesús are easy, cosmopolitan hosts who have shown enormous sensitivity in the restoration of this former *lagar* (a place where wine was made), preserving whatever they could of the original building whilst introducing bold colours (made with natural pigments brought from as far afield as Egypt and Tunisia) and modern decorative elements. The restaurant doubles as a gallery for local artists. There are five bedrooms and a guest lounge on the top two floors. Their decoration was a labour of love. There are handmade ceramic tiles and polished stucco in the bathrooms, ragged and sponged paint finishes, cut flowers, rugs from Tunisia and Afghanistan. Stay here and you'll bless the day your hosts' car broke down and they were forced to make an unscheduled stop in Gaucín.

To see and do: walking in the Gaucín area, day trip to Tangier, visits to Ronda and the white villages.

CORTIJO EL PUERTO DEL NEGRO

Apartado de Correos 25   **Map: 10**
29480 Gaucín
(Málaga)

Tel: 95 2151239 or 649 011362   **Fax:** 95 2151239

e-mail: puertodelnegro@mercuryin.es

Web Page: www.karenbrown.com

Closed: 15 November - 1 February.

Bedrooms: 2 Doubles, 2 Twins and 4 self-catering Cottages.

Prices: Double/Twin €113–123 (18700-20500 Ptas) + 7% TAX. Prices for cottages available on request.

Meals: Breakfast €8 (1250 Ptas), light Lunches €15 (2500 Ptas) excluding wine, Dinner (and Lunch on Sunday) €30 (5000 Ptas) excluding wine. Restaurant closed on Tuesdays.

Getting there: from Estepona N-340 towards Algeciras then right in Sabanillas past Manilva to Gaucín. Here left at first junction then left again at petrol station on A-369 towards Algeciras. After 2km turn right at sign for Puerto del Negro: the hotel is on the left after 1.8km.

045

Management: Christine & Tony Martin

You may just have read about El Puerto del Negro in a magazine or a newspaper somewhere on your travels. Journalists are invariably moved to hyperbole by this exceptional place and so too are those lucky enough to stay here. The position is simply out of this world – a lone perch on a last spur of the Ronda Sierra with vast views out across forests and valleys to Gibraltar and Africa. A long drive arcs up to the hotel's white frontage, its lines softened by rambling creepers, wistaria and jasmine. Exuberant gardens spill down from the surrounding terraces. Guests come for the utter tranquility and the exclusive house-party atmosphere in which the accent is placed firmly on the Better Things in Life. The food at El Puerto del Negro is as cosmopolitan and as refined as the house itself. Bedrooms have every creature comfort and, like the lounge, mix furnishings and decorative elements from Africa, India and the Far East with a hint of the Home Counties. And there's a snooker room, a tennis court and a pool placed at a discrete distance from the main house.

To see and do: train ride to Ronda, the Tarifa beaches, the Roman ruins at Bolonia, walking in the Gaucín area.

LA ALMUÑA

Apartado de Correos 20   **Map: 10**
29480 Gaucín
(Málaga)

Tel: 95 2151200   **Fax:** 95 2151343

Web Page: www.andalucia.com

Closed: Never.

Bedrooms: 3 Doubles, 1 Twin and 1 Cottage.

Prices: Double/Twin €96 (16000 Ptas), Cottage for two €730 (121500 Ptas) per week, for four €892 (148.500 Ptas) per week + 7% TAX.

Meals: Breakfast included, Dinner €24 (4000 Ptas) including wine.

Getting there: from Estepona N-340 towards Algeciras then right via Manilva to Gaucín. Here left at first junction then left again at petrol station on A-369 towards Algeciras. At km 44.8, turn left at round post into 'La Almuña' estate. Diana's is the house to right of track behind a line of cypress trees.

046

Management: Diana Paget

There is nowhere to stay in Spain quite like La Almuña, one of the few B&Bs which really does live up to the Spanish dictum of *mi casa es tu casa* (my home is your home). The life and soul of the place is Diana Paget. Hers is a relaxed, shambolic and utterly welcoming home of the take-us-as-you-find-us type. Swallows nest in the kitchen, dogs lounge on the sofas, friends pop in and out for a cup of tea, a gin and tonic or for dinner, but Diana manages to carry on with her culinary preparations unperturbed, the complete antithesis of the Forté Junior Manager. La Almuña was the main farmhouse on a large estate which is now shared by a number of (mostly British) families. From here there are incredible views out over the rolling farmlands south of Gaucín and of the distant Moroccan Rif. Although parts of the house are getting a little worn at the edges, guests return year after year to stay with Diana. They come to ride, walk, eat and talk in the very best of company.

To see and do: walking and riding in the Gaucín area, train ride to Ronda, the Tarifa beaches, and the Roman ruins at Bolonia.

HOTEL RURAL BANU RABBAH

Calle Sierra Bermeja s/n   **Map: 10**
29490 Benarrabá
(Málaga)

Tel: 95 2150288/76 or 696 968803   **Fax:** 95 2150288

e-mail: hotel@hbenarraba.es

Web Page: www.hbenarraba.es

Closed: Never.

Bedrooms: 12 Twins.

Prices: Twin €42–48 (7000–8000 Ptas) + 7% TAX.

Meals: Breakfast €2 (450 Ptas), Lunch/Dinner €9 (1450 Ptas) including wine.

Getting there: from Estepona N-340 towards Algeciras then right via Manilva to Gaucín. Here right towards Ronda on the A-369. After 4.5km turn right down hill to Benarrabá. Hotel is at far end of village next to municipal pool.

047

Management: Jesús García

Although Benarrabá is just a couple of miles from Gaucín, few foreigners visit the village and there are just a handful of ex-pat residents. Yet this is an archetypical white village with gorgeous vistas out across the chestnut and oak forests of the Genal valley. At the far side of the village, alone on a spur next to the municipal sport's ground, Hotel Banu Rabbah is beginning to establish a reputation amongst the walking community as a friendly, comfortable and very well-priced sleep-over. Although the building would win no prizes for its architecture, plants are beginning to soften its angular lines and half of the bedrooms, as well as the lounge/reception area, look out across the valley. They are decorated with hand-painted wooden beds, tables and dressers and have large, arched terraces. The hotel's restaurant is just 25 yards from the main building, next to the village swimming pool, not a venue for a gourmet extravaganza but rather for simple dinners which look to the local recipe books for their inspiration. The staff are young and friendly and the walking here is fantastic.

To see and do: walking in the Genal Valley, visits to the Pileta Cave, Gaucín and Ronda and the white villages.

EL GECKO

Calle Cañada Real del Tesoro   **Map: 10**
29391 Estación de Cortes de la Frontera
(Málaga)

Tel: 95 2153315   **Fax:** 95 2153266

e-mail: elgecko@mercuryin.es

Web Page: www.andalucia.com

Closed: January & February.

Bedrooms: 3 Doubles and 2 Twins.

Prices: Double/Twin €72 (12000 Ptas) including TAX.

Meals: Breakfast included, Lunch/Dinner €18–24 (3000–4000 Ptas) including wine.

Getting there: from Ronda A-376 towards Sevilla then left to Benaoján. There towards Montejaque then left towards Cortes de la Frontera. As you arrive in Cortes take sharp left turn signposted for Gaucín and go down hill to Estación de Cortes: El Gecko is signposted to the right just before you cross the river.

048

Management: Rachel Dring

Rachel's name may ring a bell if you have stayed at the Casablanca in Gaucín. Daughter of Mike and Sue, she managed the restaurant there for several years before opening her own small hotel right next to the river in the sleepy, railroad village of Estación de Cortes. She is brilliantly suited to her role of mine host – relaxed, caring and with the ability to make her staff feel a valued part of the big picture, one of the secrets of making a success of any small hotel. She also has a designer's feel for colour and design. The hotel's gecko motif is her work and seems to capture the optimistic, cheerful mood of the place. Much of its intimacy and high feel-good factor comes from the warm creamy-lemon colour scheme which is nicely contrasted by dark beams and lime-coloured chairs in the dining room and by richly-coloured bedspreads and cushions in the bedrooms. The dining areas and four of the five (large) bedrooms look river-wards. You'll hear birdsong rather than passing traffic. Everyone who stays here has only good things to say about Rachel, her cooking and El Gecko.

To see and do: walking in the Alcornocales and Grazalema Natural Parks, visits to the Pileta Cave, Ronda and the white villages.

MOLINO DEL SANTO

Barriada de la Estación **Map: 10**
29370 Benaoján
(Málaga)

Tel: 95 2167151 **Fax:** 95 2167327

e-mail: molino@logiccontrol.es

Web Page: www.andalucia.com/molino

Closed: 17 November – 15 February.

Bedrooms: 1 Single, 7 Doubles, 7 Twins and 2 Suites.

Prices: Single €53–96 (8805–15915 Ptas), Double/Twin €68–104 (11360–17230 Ptas), Suite €93–129 (15510–21500 Ptas) including TAX. Half-board obligatory during High Season.

Meals: Breakfast included, Lunch €9–12 (1500-2000 Ptas) including wine, Dinner €24 (4000 Ptas) including wine.

Getting there: From Ronda A-376 towards Sevilla then left on MA-555 towards Benaoján. After 12km, cross railway and river bridges then turn left to Estación de Benaoján and follow signs to El Molino.

049

Management: Pauline Elkin & Andy Chapell

Wherever I travel in Andalucía, I seem to meet with someone who enthuses to me about El Molino del Santo. Pauline Elkin and Andy Chapell have gradually built the place up to model-small-hotel status thanks to more than a decade of hard work and good will. The physical setting is magnificent – right beside a rushing mountain torrent that once powered the mill's waterwheels, surrounded by exuberant vegetation and with views out to the rocky hillsides of the Guadiaro valley. Guests return time and time again because of the friendliness of the staff and the reassurance of known-standards in El Molino's restaurant (one of the first in the area to make real efforts to buy organically-grown produce) and in its bedrooms which are redecorated and improved at the end of every season. Andy and Pauline's hotel is the proof that ethics and business are happy bedfellows. Come here to walk, to visit Ronda and the white villages or just to relax beneath the willows to the sound of that wonderful rushing water. But be sure to book your room as soon as possible.

To see and do: the Pileta Cave, walking in the Grazalema Natural Park, visits to Ronda and the white villages.

EL HORCAJO

Apartado de Correos 149 **Map: 10**
29400 Ronda
(Málaga)

Tel: 95 2184080   **Fax:** 95 2184171

e-mail: info@elhorcajo.com

Web Page: www.elhorcajo.com

Closed: Never

Bedrooms: 1 Double, 11 Twins and 10 Duplex rooms (with 1 double and 2 singles) sleeping up to 4.

Prices: Double/Twin €69 (11500 Ptas), Duplex for 2 €82 (13600 Ptas) + 7 % TAX.

Meals: Breakfast included, Lunch/Dinner €14 (2300 Ptas) excluding wine.

Getting there: from Ronda A-376 towards Sevilla. After approximately 15km turn left at signs for Grazalema. Don't take next left turn for Grazalema but rather continue on towards Zahara. El Horcajo is signposted to the left of the road: follow a long track down to the farm in floor of valley.

050

Management: Antonio Jesús Reina

It´s amazing how many small hotels have opened in the Ronda mountains in the past three or four years, evidence of the growing numbers of visitors to the area and of the substantial grants that have poured in from Brussels. El Horcajo was once a lowly cattle farm but has been given a new role in life thanks to the dynamism of owner Luis González. You reach the farm by winding down to the bottom of a deep valley that lies on the northern boundary of the Grazalema Natural Park. Heavy wooden doors lead through into the huge, vaulted lounge (the former cattle byre). Just off to one side is the beamed dining room where simple, country-style cuisine is the keynote. Every last corner of the place has been decorated in traditional andalusian rustic style with beams and terracotta floor tiles, cobbled courtyard, and wooden Ronda-style bedroom furniture. The quietest rooms in the main farmhouse are those that give onto the inner patio where a huge mulberry provides welcome shade in summer. The rooms in a newly added annex are mezzanine style, great for a family. And Ronda and Grazalema are within driving distance.

To see and do: walking in the Grazalema Natural Park, visits to Ronda and the white villlages, and the Pileta Cave.

EL TEJAR

Calle Nacimiento   **Map: 10**
29430 Montecorto
(Málaga)

Tel: 95 2184053   **Fax:** 95 2184053

e-mail: eltejar@mercuryin.es

Web Page: www.sawdays.co.uk

Closed: mid-June – end of August.

Bedrooms: 2 Twins and 1 Double with own lounge.

Prices: Twin €57 (9500 Ptas), Double €63 (10500 Ptas) including TAX.

Meals: Breakfast €4 (600 Ptas), Dinner €20 (3250 Ptas) including wine.

Getting there: from Ronda take A-376 to Montecorto. As you arrive in village take cobbled track just to right of *ayuntamiento* signposted 'Bar La Piscina'. At end of track turn right, pass to the left of house no.54. Pass 2 more houses then go sharp right up track through pines then bear right to El Tejar.

051

Management: Emma Baverstock & Guy Hunter-Watts

Andalucía at its most seductive! A whitewashed house, the very highest in the village, festooned with bougainvillaea, honeysuckle and jasmine. Cobbles and terracotta. A sweeping panorama of mountain, wheat fields and forest. And interior design and décor that evokes Andalucía's Moorish past in both lounge and bedrooms. Pointed arches, bright Moroccan kilims, deep ochre colour washes. If you're looking for a place to wind down, then look no further. Pour yourself a drink from the honesty bar whilst the friendliest of spaniels looks languidly on, browse through one of several hundred books on Spain, put on a CD and slip into one of the most relaxed B&B set-ups in Spain. The sound of water in a spring-fed pool lulls you at siesta time whilst at breakfast the sound of flamenco, fado, jazz, blues or baroque music accompanies freshly-squeezed orange juice and pot-fulls of coffee. Ride with Emma up to an amazing Roman theatre hewn out of solid rock, walk with Guy along forgotten mountain paths and then return to your large, airy room-with-a-view.

To see and do: walking and riding in the Grazalema Natural Park, visits to the Roman theatre of Accinipo, the Pileta Cave, Ronda and the white villages.

CORTIJO PUERTO LLANO

Apartado de Correos 224
29400 Ronda
(Málaga)

Map: 10

Tel: 95 2114227   **Fax:** 95 2114227

e-mail: cortijoronda@yahoo.es

Web Page: www.andalucia.com

Closed: Never.

Bedrooms: 1 Single and 3 Twins.

Prices: Single €54 (9000 Ptas), Twin €84 (14000 Ptas) including TAX.

Meals: Breakfast €6 (1000 Ptas), no Lunch/Dinner available: plenty of choice in Ronda which is just 15 minutes from Puerto Llano.

Getting there: from Ronda take the A-376 towards Sevilla. After 9kms turn right on the MA-499 towards Ronda La Vieja. The road climbs and then levels: the entrance to Cortijo Puerto Llano is on the right next to km8 marker post.

052

Management: Aart van Kruiselbergen & Michael Cox

Cortijo Puerto Llano sits high on a hilltop above Ronda, a short walk from the Roman ruins of Accinipo whose theatre, hewn out of solid rock, is simply amazing yet attracts curiously few visitors. Aart and Michael have lived long in Spain. Both are artists and its easy to see why they should have fallen in love with Puerto Llano, its whitewashed walls contrasted by the fields of wheat and sunflowers that lap right up to the house. The house has been decorated with an artist's eye for detail. It feels simply elegant with a minimum of clutter and, of course, there are masses of paintings and drawings. A large guest lounge, reached by way of paths flanked by clipped hedges of rosemary, doubles as a gallery for Aart and Michael's work and the bedrooms, giving onto the cobbled inner patio, are also brightened by their paintings. You couldn't hope to meet with kinder hosts and although only breakfast is on offer, Ronda is just 15 minutes away. There is also a fully-equipped kitchen if you prefer to prepare your own meals.

To see and do: Roman theatre of Accinipo, Ronda, the white villages, and Setenil de las Bodegas.

LA FUENTE DE LA HIGUERA

Partido de los Frontones   **Map: 10**
29400 Ronda
(Málaga)

Tel: 95 2114355 or 610 847731   **Fax:** 95 2114356

e-mail: info@hotellafuente.com

Web Page: www.hotellafuente.com

Closed: 1-22 December.

Bedrooms: 3 Twins, 1 larger Double, 5 Suites for 2, 1 Suite for 4 and 1 Apartment.

Prices: Twin €99 (16500 Ptas), larger Double/Apartment €129 (21500 Ptas), Suite for two €138–150 (23000–25000 Ptas), Suite for four €189 (31500 Ptas) + 7% TAX.

Meals: Breakfast included, light Lunches €9 (1500 Ptas), Dinner €27 (4500 Ptas) excluding wine.

Getting there: from San Pedro de Alcantara A-376 bypassing Ronda towards Sevilla. Shortly past the turning for Benaoján (don´t take this road!) between km posts 116 and 117 turn right. Go under bridge and then left at first fork. Cross a small bridge and after approx. 200 metres left again at sign for hotel.

053

Management: Christina & Pom Piek

Two years ago, when Pom and Tina decided to convert a tumble-down olive mill, everyone else was opting for Andalusian country style. But they were after something spicier, something different. So whole floors were shipped in from the Far East, there's not a twisted beam in sight and, where others might have hung a print of the Ronda bridge, there's modern art from Amsterdam. What they've achieved is a light, airy, exceptionally soothing series of spaces that also seem imbued with the laid-back spirit of the owners. The travel magazine Condé Nast seemed to get a finger on the pulse of the place when they wrote about the "chilled-out, house-party atmosphere". The hotel stands high on a hill surrounded by a vast olive grove with views out across the pool to Ronda. At night it is simply magical here. Bedrooms (most of them suites) are huge and colonial-style furniture is nicely contrasted against their clean lines. The food is good, the selection of wines excellent and the hotel has a growing number of loyal clients. So be sure to book early.

To see and do: riding and walking in the Grazalema and Sierra de las Nieves Natural Parks, ballooning near Ronda, visits to Ronda town and the white villages.

HOTEL SAN GABRIEL

Calle Marqués de Moctezuma 19   **Map: 10**
29400 Ronda
(Málaga)

Tel: 95 2190392 **Fax:** 95 2190117

e-mail: info@hotelsangabriel.com

Web Page: www.hotelsangabriel.com

Closed: 2 weeks in January after Epiphany.

Bedrooms: 9 Doubles, 6 Twins and 1 Suite.

Prices: Double/Twin €72 (12000 Ptas), Suite €84 (14000 Ptas) + 7% TAX.

Meals: Breakfast €4 (700 Ptas), no Lunch/Dinner available: several good restaurants and tapas bars close to hotel.

Getting there: from San Pedro de Alcántara A-376 to Ronda. Take the first entrance into the town. Pass in front of the old town walls and then bear right and upwards into the old town. Here take the second street on the left. The hotel is next to the Plaza del Gigante. First leave your bags at the hotel (the staff will help you) and then park in the plaza.

054

Management: José Manuel Arnal Pérez

The owners like to describe San Gabriel as *un pequeño gran hotel,* a great little hotel. They're right. A stay here is somehow "greater" than the normal hotel experience. This exceptionally kind Ronda family make you feel not only an honoured guest but also like a friend of the family. I remember meeting a family who emerged from their room to find presents under the tree for them on Christmas day! The hotel is at the very heart of the old town of Ronda, just yards from that awesome gorge and bridge. This is every inch the grand, seigneurial town house – coat-of-arms above an entrance of dressed stone, wonderful old wrought-iron grilles wrapped about by a rampant honeysuckle, and a grand sweep of staircase (rescued from the old town hall) leading up to the bedrooms. There's the most inviting of lounges with masses of books, magazines, rugs, tapestries and family photos. Just beyond is a billiards room and a tiny "cinema" where you can watch one of your favourite oldies on video. The bedrooms are to write home about and there's a cellar bar for pre-dinner tapas and a fino.

To see and do: the Mondragón Palace, Plaza de Toros, La Casa del Rey Moro, and La Mina (the mine).

Málaga Province

ALAVERÁ DE LOS BAÑOS

Calle San Miguel s/n   **Map: 10**
29400 Ronda
(Málaga)

Tel: 95 2879143   **Fax:** 95 2879143

e-mail: alavera@ctv.es

Web Page: www.andalucia.com

Closed: 18 November – 3 December and 23 December – 8 January.

Bedrooms: 1 Single, 7 Doubles and 3 Twins.

Prices: Single €42 (7000 Ptas), Double/Twin €54–66 (9000–11000 Ptas) including TAX.

Meals: Breakfast included, Lunch/Dinner €18–21 (3000–3500 Ptas) including wine.

Getting there: from San Pedro take A-376 to Ronda. Go through the old town, cross the bridge and directly opposite Parador right into Calle Villanueva. Right at the end, down hill to the Fuente de los Ocho Caños. Left here and then first right down hill and cross bridge to the Arab Baths; hotel next door.

055

Management: Inmaculada Villanueva Ayala & Christian Reichardt

Alavera de los Baños literally means "by the side of the Arab Baths" and this small hotel stands cheek-by-jowel with what is probably Andalusia's best preserved "hammam" (arabic term for a bath house). When Christian and Inma, the hotel's young owners, first set eyes on the place, there was just a crumbling ruin here, but thanks to masses of hard work and the savoir-faire of a local architect, Alavera has become a favourite stopover with a popular restaurant whose culinary slant is towards the flavours of north Africa. The decorative style of the dining room and the bedrooms is evocative, too, of Andalusia's Moorish past. Kilims, lamps and mosaic-topped tables were shipped in from the Maghreb and the colour washes are reminiscent of the earthy colours of that part of the world. Bedrooms are small but the space has been imaginatively used: showers rather than baths and small sinks with handmade ceramic tiles were an attractive and practical space-saving solution. What you most remember after a stay here is the easy, relaxed manner of Christian and Inma who make a stay here doubly special.

To see and do: the Arab baths, Plaza de Toros, La Casa del Rey Moro and La Mina (the mine).

AMANHAVIS HOTEL

Calle del Pilar 3   **Map: 10**
29679 Benahavis
(Málaga)

Tel: 95 2856026   **Fax:** 95 2856151

e-mail: info@amanhavis.com

Web Page: www.amanhavis.com

Closed: 7 January – 3 February.

Bedrooms: 3 Doubles, 3 Twins and 3 Deluxe rooms.

Prices: Double/Twin €105–147 (17500–24500 Ptas), Deluxe rooms €135–165 (22500–27500 Ptas) + 7% TAX.

Meals: Breakfast €11 (1750 Ptas), Dinner €30 (4950 Ptas) excluding wine. Restaurant closed Sunday & Monday and from 7 January– 12 February 2002.

Getting there: from San Pedro take the N-340 towards Algeciras and then turn right for Benahavis. Follow road all the way through village; after road turns sharp right continue 25m and turn left and Amanhavis is on your left.

056

Management: Burkhard Weber

Anyone living in the Marbella area will have heard of Benahavis. This attractive medieval village, reached by way of a spectacular gorge that cuts in from the N-340, is a popular gastronomic destination amongst locals, ex-pats and holidaymakers who come to eat at one of the several restaurants that line its narrow streets. The owners of Amanhavis wanted to create something with a rather different feel and thanks to their savoir-faire and imagination their small hotel now numbers amongst Andalucia's most original places to stay. The bedrooms are an extraordinary flight of fantasy, each one of them with a different historical theme inspired by Spain's medieval period and with decoration to match. In the Astronomer's Observatory you can look up to the stars from your pillow, Sultan Boabdil's chamber feels plucked from One Thousand and One Nights whilst the Catholic Kings' chamber has a more regal air. The rooms wrap round a romantic inner courtyard and plunge pool where you feast on inspired, Mediterranean cuisine accompanied by a selection of both Spanish and international wines.

To see and do: golf, beaches, Puerto Banus and Marbella.

HOTEL POSADA DEL CANÓNIGO

Calle Mesones 24   **Map: 11**
29420 El Burgo
(Málaga)

Tel: 95 2160185   **Fax:** 95 2160185

Closed: 24 December.

Bedrooms: 7 Doubles and 5 Twins.

Prices: Double/Twin €44–51 (7270–8415 Ptas) including TAX.

Meals: Breakfast included, Lunch/Dinner €9 (1500 Ptas) excluding wine.

Getting there: from Marbella A-355 to Coín and there take A-366 to El Burgo. There head for village centre signposted "casco urbano" and pick up signs for the Posada del Canónigo. Hotel is on right as you head up Calle Mesones.

057

Management: María Reyes

If you're heading up to Ronda from Málaga and don't mind the odd hairpin bend, be sure to take the inland route via El Burgo. After cutting through the irrigated valleys around Coín you climb up to a much wilder, starker swathe of mountains where eagles ride the winds and where bandaleros once plied their trade. Nowadays you'd be unlucky to be held up by anyone other than a zealous *guardía civil* – yet El Burgo still feels as though the 21st century has passed it by. And if you enjoy old-fashioned hospitality, this immensely friendly, family-run posada – the fruit of the conversion of an 18th century village house – should be your first choice. The heart of the hotel is its wonderfully intimate dining room where a fire always burns in the colder months and where you dine on simple, traditional country food. The framed cross-stitch, low beams, and unrendered walls feel plucked from another age. And the bedrooms, many of which have views out to the mountains, feel just as authentic with their beams, lace curtains, antique beds and terracotta floors. A very favourite address.

To see and do: walking in the Sierra de las Nieves Natural Park, horse-riding, visits to Ronda and the white villages.

HOTEL LA CASA GRANDE DEL BURGO

Calle Mesones 1   **Map: 11**
29420 El Burgo
(Málaga)

Tel: 95 2160232   **Fax:** 95 2160181

e-mail: hotelcasagrande@hotel-casagrande.com

Web Page: www.hotel-casagrande.com

Closed: Never.

Bedrooms: 13 Doubles and 5 Twins.

Prices: Standard Double/Twin €48–54 (7900–8935 Ptas),
superior Double €51–65 (8410–10721 Ptas) including TAX.

Meals: Breakfast included, Dinner €9 (1500 Ptas) excluding
wine.

Getting there: from Marbella A-355 to Coín and there take A-
366 to El Burgo. There head for village centre signposted
"casco urbano" and pick up signs for the Casa Grande: on the
left as you reach Calle Mesones.

058

Management: Juan Antonio González Ramirez

It's a sign of changing times in the *Serranía* that whichever small mountain village you now should choose to visit, you'll invariably come across a newly opened hotel. The same holds true for El Burgo and La Casa Grande, a 150-year-old village house that has been extensively renovated, with its fair quota of EEC grants, to create a surprisingly luxurious small hotel. Many of the house's original features were saved, such as doors, roof beams, floor tiles, ornate mouldings and chimney pieces. Everything else is brand-spanking new, most notably the beautiful carved wooden furniture in the bedrooms and handsome repro taps in their bathrooms. Although they're smaller and you sacrifice bath for shower, I'd choose one of the bedrooms that horseshoe round a patio to the rear of the house that look out over the village's rooftops (numbers 6-12). Warm colour washes help create a mood of welcome throughout the hotel, the staff are exceptionally friendly and both food and rooms are brilliant value.

To see and do: walking in the Sierra de las Nieves Natural Park, horse-riding, visits to Ronda and the white villages.

HOTEL LA ERA

Partido Martina
Los Cerrillos, parcela 85
29566 Casarabonela
(Málaga)

Map: 11

Tel: 95 2112525 or 95 2112538   **Fax:** 95 2112009

e-mail: laera@wol.es

Web Page: www.laera.cjb.es

Closed: 22 December – 7 January.

Bedrooms: 5 Doubles and 4 Twins.

Prices: Double/Twin €90 (15000 Ptas) including TAX.

Meals: Breakfast included, Dinner €18 (2950 Ptas) excluding wine.

Getting there: from airport take the N-340 round Málaga then exit for Cártama/Universidad on A-357. Bypass Cártama then exit on MA-403 towards Casarabonela. Just before you reach village right at signs for La Era: follow signs for 2kms to hotel.

059

Management: Isabel Manrara Díaz

I had the good fortune to stumble upon La Era when headed homewards through the mountains east of Ronda. My hotel appetite is always wetted by any approach that promises to get me away from civilisation, and when I rounded a final bend and came up to La Era, high on a spur of the mountains across from beautiful Casarabonela, I sensed that this was going to be a memorable night away. Lydia and Paco left no stone unturned in their quest to create a truly special country hotel. Taps, beds, fabrics, mattresses, doors, sheets, towels are all are top-of-the-range and no detail has been forgotten by Lydia whose pride in her hotel is tangible – and justified. She also happens to be an exceptionally good cook and although I arrived unannounced she managed to magic up a delicious meal in next-to-no-time (normally menus are discussed and tailored to your tastes) and the extent of her breakfast buffet will have you forgetting about lunch. Add to all this a comfortable lounge, a genuinely friendly welcome, amazing views and you should begin to get a feel for the place.

To see and do: El Chorro lakes and gorge, the pinsapo forest near Yunquera, the spa town of Carratraca.

EL MOLINO SANTISTEBAN

A-366 km 52-53   **Map: 11**
Apartado de Correos 86
29100 Guaro
(Málaga)

Tel: 95 2453748 or 687 679021

e-mail: info@elmolinosantisteban.com

Web Page: www.hotelmolino.com

Closed: Never.

Bedrooms: 3 Doubles and 3 Twins.

Prices: Double/Twin €51–63 (8500-10500 Ptas) + 7% TAX.

Meals: Breakfast included, no Lunch/Dinner available: 2 restaurants very close and plenty of choice in Coín.

Getting there: From Málaga airport N-340 towards Cádiz and almost immediateley turn right at signpost for Coín. Here take A-366 towards Ronda. Molino Santisteban is just to the right of the road, between km marker posts 52 and 53 .

060

Management: Frits Blomsma

Frits and Gisele are amongst a growing number of young Europeans who have headed south in search of a better life in the hills of Andalucía. Visit them and you'll understand why they should have fallen for this old mill house which stands amongst groves of citrus and fields of almonds and avocados in the fertile valley of the Río Grande. Santisteban's architecture is rather reminiscent of a hacienda but on a smaller scale. The six bedrooms give onto a sheltered inner patio where a gurgling fountain and birdsong is about all that you'll hear at siesta time. The dining room, just across from the main building, offers cool respite during the hotter months and a cosy retreat in winter where guests breakfast round a magnificent antique almond-wood table. Orange juice is always squeezed fresh from Santisteban's own fruit and there are cheeses and meats, jams and cereals, yoghurts and eggs to set you up for the day should you head out for a hike along the valley or venture up into the Serranía de las Nieves Natural Park. And there are two good restaurants just yards from the front gate.

To see and do: walking in the Sierra de las Nieves Natural Park, visits to Ronda and the white villages.

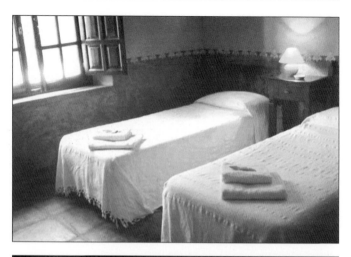

SANTA FE

Ctra de Monda km 3   **Map: 11**
29100 Coín
(Málaga)

Tel: 95 2452916   **Fax:** 95 2453843

e-mail: info@santafe-hotel.com

Web Page: www.santafe-hotel.com

Closed: 2 weeks in November and 2 weeks in January/February.

Bedrooms: 5 Twins.

Prices: Twin €61 (10165 Ptas) including TAX.

Meals: Breakfast included, Lunch €15 (2500 Ptas), Dinner €21 (3500 Ptas) excluding wine.

Getting there: from Málaga to Coín. As you arrive in Coín follow signs towards Marbella/Monda. Santa Fe is on the right after 3kms.

061

Management: Warden & Arjan van de Vrande

Santa Fe could be just the place to stay if you are wanting a sea and mountain holiday. You can be on the beach in just half an hour and the Sierra de las Nieves is right on your doorstep, too. The hotel is just to one side of the road that cuts through the hills between Coín and Marbella, an old farmhouse surrounded by the groves of citrus fruit that line the Guadalhorce valley. The focus of the place in the warmer months is the poolside terrace (where a huge olive tree provides welcome shade) whilst when temperatures drop a warmly decorated, beamed dining room is a wonderfully intimate spot for your meals. Foodies will enjoy Santa Fe. The young Dutch owners Arjan and Warden have built up a solid reputation for their mix of Andalusian and International food and lots of people drive up from the coast to eat here. Amongst the specialities are crayfish with spinach, sirloin of lamb *al vino de Jerez* and wonderful Dutch-style apple pie. The beamed, terracotta-tiled bedrooms are inviting, too, and have recently been completely redecorated.

To see and do: horse-riding, walking in the Sierra de la Nieves Natural Park, visits to Puerto Banus, Marbella and beaches.

HACIENDA DE SAN JOSÉ

Buzón 59
Entrerrios
29650 Mijas
(Málaga)

Map: 11

Tel: 95 2119494   **Fax:** 95 2119404

e-mail: haciendasanjose@yahoo.co.uk

Web Page: www.hotelruralhaciendasanjose.com

Closed: 1 June - 31 August.

Bedrooms: 5 large Twins (Junior Suites)

Prices: Twin €117 (19500 Ptas) + 7% TAX.

Meals: Breakfast included, Dinner €17–21 (2800–3500 Ptas) excluding wine. Restaurant closed Monday evenings.

Getting there: from Fuengirola take the N-340 towards Marbella. In Cala de Mijas turn right at signs "Campo de Golf". Turn right at the first roundabout then at the next fork turn right again towards Entrerrios. The hotel is signposted on the left after 1.8km.

062

Management: Nicky & José García

Nicky and José built and managed a successful tennis club before seeing a more peaceful future in their own small country-house hotel. As past hoteliers and travellers, too, they knew exactly what they were after, a truly comfortable home-from-home in a peaceful and rural location yet still close to the Costa del Sol. As you follow the steep drive up to this hacienda style building, it's hard to imagine that a couple of years back this was a bare hillside. Oleander, cypress, olive, palm and plumbago are already taking root and a sea of colour laps up to the house's front door. The five guest rooms are set around a pebbled inner courtyard where a fountain murmurs. It feels almost cloister-like. Your room will be huge, airy and light. Each has its own terrace, an enormous bathroom, fitted wardrobes and top-of-the-range linen and mattresses. You won't sleep more comfortably than here. Up a level is a large lounge, a cosy library and a brightly decorated dining room. You eat well at San José and you won't want for good wine: Pepe has a well-stocked cellar and will soon be harvesting the first grapes for his own *Gran Reserva*!

To see and do: nearby beaches, golf, visits to Mijas pueblo, Puerto Banus and Marbella.

THE BEACH HOUSE

Urbanización El Chaparral   **Map: 11**
Ctra de Cádiz N-340 km 203
29648 Mijas Costa
(Málaga)

Tel: 95 2494540   **Fax:** 95 2494540

e-mail: info@beachhouse.nu

Web Page: www.beachhouse.nu

Closed: Never.

Bedrooms: 5 Doubles, 4 Twins and I larger Double.

Prices: Double/Twin €108 (18000 Ptas), larger Double €144 (24000 Ptas) including TAX.

Meals: Breakfast included, no Lunch/Dinner available: lots of local and international restaurants a short drive from the Beach House.

Getting there: from airport N-340 towards Cádiz then right onto A-7. At fork follow signs for Fuengirola/ Mijas: you rejoin the N-340. Pass km post 202 and after approx. 600m exit for Calas de Mijas. Take N-340 back towards Fuengirola. Immediately after footbridge exit on slip road to The Beach House.

063

Management: Kjell Sporrong & Olof Naslund

After a recent change of owners and complete decorative metamorphosis, The Beach House now numbers amongst Andalucía's most stylish small hotels. Kjell and Olof previously worked in the world of design in Stockholm and every last corner of their Andalusian villa has been decorated with aesthetic appeal in mind. There's a hint of nineties minimalism, a definite debt to things Japanese and an overall feel of repose for body and mind in both the lounge-diner and in the bedrooms. The main protagonists here are the sea and the sky, their colours changing with each passing hour. The Mediterranean laps up to within yards of the Beach House and its pool and terrace almost seem to fuse with the ocean. The best rooms here are naturally those with sea views: the busy N-340 runs close to the other side of the house and you hear passing traffic from these rooms. Olof and Kjell are charming, cosmopolitan hosts and prepare a wonderful buffet breakfast which will include a glass of chilled cava at the weekend. They will, of course, direct you towards the best local restaurants.

To see and do: watersports, beaches, horse-riding, golf, visits to Mijas pueblo and Marbella

LAS ISLAS

Calle Canela 12   **Map: 11**
Torreblanca del Sol
29640 Fuengirola
(Málaga)

Tel: 95 2475598 or 608 954448   **Fax:** 95 2464298

e-mail: zizielo@terra.es

Web Page: www.costadelsol.spa.es/hotel/lasislas

Closed: Mid November - early March.

Bedrooms: 2 Singles, 4 Doubles and 6 Twins.

Prices: Single €36 (6000 Ptas), Double/Twin €60 (10000 Ptas) + 7% TAX.

Meals: Breakfast included, Light Lunches €6 (1000 Ptas) excluding wine, Dinner €27 (4500 Ptas) including wine. Restaurant closed on Mondays.

Getting there: from airport take N-340 towards Algeciras. Bypass Torremolinos, continue on through Benalmádena Costa then Carabajal to Torreblanca. Here, just as you pass a chemists, turn right at roundabout and follow the blue signs to the hotel.

064

Management: Ghislaine & Hardy Honig

Who would ever guess that places like this could exist less than a mile from the sprawling development of Andalucía's battered Costa? Ghislaine's parents bought this tiny, hidden glade nearly 40 years ago when few people had heard of Fuengirola. A villa and rooms were built and a wonderful garden planted: it feels more like being in the Tropics when you contemplate the jacaranda, date palms, cypress and banana trees which make such a wonderful backdrop to the large swimming pool. The 12 guest rooms look out onto all this greenery and one or two of them catch a view of the sea. Their decoration feels fresh and simple – nothing fancy but then nothing's missing, either, and all of them have balconies. You'll awake here to a chorus of birdsong rather than to the sound of a TV in the next room (in fact, there are no TVs here). But the heart and soul of Las Islas is its restaurant. Hardy's food is first-class, with a definite debt to things French and German, and you couldn't wish for a more charming hostess than Ghislaine who greets you with the kindest of smiles.

To see and do: golf, horse-riding, watersports, visit to Mijas pueblo.

FINCA BLAKE

Ctra Mijas-Fuengirola km 2   **Map: 11**
29650 Mijas Pueblo
(Málaga)

Tel: 95 2590401   **Fax:** 95 2590401

Web Page: www.specialplacestostay.com

Closed: Never.

Bedrooms: 1 Double, 1 Twin and 1 Cottage sleeping 3.

Prices: Double/Twin/Cottage for two €66–72 (11000–12000 Ptas) including TAX.

Meals: Breakfast included, no Lunch/Dinner available: stacks of good restaurants in and around Mijas.

Getting there: from Málaga take N-340 towards Cádiz and then filter on to A-7. Leave motorway at exit 213 for Mijas and Fuengirola and then take the A-387 up the hill towards Mijas Pueblo. Pass the "Molino del Cura" restaurant and Finca Blake is signposted just to the left of the road.

065

Management: Amélie Pommier

Mijas is just a few miles inland from the Costa and although a huge number of ex-pats live in and around the village it has retained much of its Andalusian character. The best time to visit is at night when the views down to the twinkling resort towns are truly spectacular. Years ago Finca Blake belonged to a retired English major who caused a minor sensation when he arrived in Mijas one year... by car! Amélie fell in love with the place and for many years has continued to nurture the house's extraordinary garden where there are no less than a thousand different species. She runs Finca Blake in the best tradition of B&B: the intimacy of guests is respected whilst advice on where to eat or visit is always there should you ask. Her rooms feel like those of a private home and are decorated with oil paintings, rugs, antique dressers and masses of knick-knacks. Breakfast (continental with good tea) is served on the terrace or in a cosy dining room. Finca Blake is close to restaurants, golf courses, the airport and the beach.

To see and do: golf, horse-riding, watersports, exploring Mijas pueblo.

CASA RURAL DOMINGO

Arroyo Cansino 4
29500 Álora
(Málaga)

Map: 11

Tel: 95 2119744 **Fax:** 95 2119744

e-mail: casadomingo@airtel.net

Web Page: www.casaruraldomingo.com

Closed: December & January.

Bedrooms: 2 doubles, 1 large Apartment and 2 Studios.

Prices: Double €48–54 (8000–9000 Ptas), Apartment €481 (80000 Ptas) weekly, Studio €361 (60000 Ptas) weekly including TAX.

Meals: Breakfast €6 (1000 Ptas), no Lunch/Dinner available: good restaurants and tapas bars a short drive away in Álora.

Getting there: from Málaga take the A-357 towards Campillos via Cártama. 16km after Cártama turn right towards Álora. At T junction turn right then after 200m left. At the next junction follow signs along the track to Casa Rural Domingo.

066

Management: Cynthia & Domien Doms

Dom and Cynthia are another young couple who have migrated south to set up a small B&B in the mountains of Málaga. They used to run a bar in Belgium and are well used to coping with a constant stream of visitors: they manage to do so with a vitality and enthusiasm that is both genuine and infectious. They built the home of their dreams on a hillside above Álora, from where there are exhilarating views down across the town and to the mountains stretching west towards Ronda. The garden has been sculpted round a large pool and just to one side is a tennis court and boules pitch. The place would be great for a family holiday and there's a barbecue area that guests are welcome to use. Most of the year breakfast is served out on the terrace. Dom busies around helping to organise your day and, if you like, can help you search out your own dream home in the valley. There are several places where you can get a good dinner in Álora and Casa Domingo is well placed for trips to both the mountains and the coast.

To see and do: horse-riding, visits to the Ardales Natural Park, El Torcal Natural Park and Antequera.

CORTIJO VALVERDE

Apartado de Correos 47   **Map: 11**
29500 Álora
(Málaga)

Tel: 95 2112979 or 627 091835   **Fax:** 95 2112979

e-mail: cortijovalverde@mercuryin.es

Web Page: www.cortijovalverde.com

Closed: Never.

Bedrooms: 3 Doubles and 4 Twins.

Prices: Double/Twin €66–75 (11000–12500 Ptas) + 7% TAX.

Meals: Breakfast included, Light Lunches €6 (1000 Ptas), Dinner €16 (2700 Ptas) excluding wine. Restaurant closed Mon, Wed and Fri night.

Getting there: from Málaga A-357 towards Campillos then right for Álora. Right at junction and after 300 yards left for Álora. Cross river and at junction by bar 'Los Caballos' turn left towards Valle de Abalajís. Pass km36 post and bus shelter then right towards Tierra Nueva. After 200m sharp left uphill to Valverde.

067

Management: Moyra & Rod Cridland

Heading north from Álora towards the amazing Torcal Natural Park, you follow the narrowest of country roads that meanders its way through fields of wheat and groves of olives and almonds. You sense that you are headed for the heart of that much touted "real" Spain. When Rod and Moyra bought this smallholding, there was just a tumble-down farmstead here, but after 18 months of building, the country inn of their dreams is up and running. Little remains of the old farm apart from a cobbled *era* (threshing circle) which, like the present house, catches the breezes that are funnelled along the valley. The most remarkable feature of Valverde is the enormous pool that lies between the main house and five of the guest rooms (20 lengths of this pool and you'll have earned your supper). And an excellent supper it will be. Rod modestly describes his oven-based creations as "good, honest food" and he drives all the way to Antequera to buy fresh vegetables. His and Moyra's enthusiasm for their adopted country is refreshing and you can bet they'll succeed at Valverde.

To see and do: visits to El Chorro gorge, the towns of Antequera and Álora, and El Torcal Natural Park.

CASA DE ELROND

Barrio Seco s/n
29230 Villanueva de la Concepción
(Málaga)

Map: 12

Tel: 95 2754091 or 689 939840   **Fax:** 95 2754091

e-mail: elrond@mercuryin.es

Closed: Never.

Bedrooms: 1 Double, 1 Twin and 1 Triple.

Prices: Double/Twin €39 (6500 Ptas). Minimum stay 2 nights.

Meals: Breakfast included, no Lunch/Dinner available: some good, simple 'ventas' a short drive away in Villanueva.

Getting there: round Málaga on the N-340 then N-331 towards Antequera/Granada. At km 241 exit for Casabermeja. Enter village, go to top of hill and at junction turn right at signs for Villanueva de la C. Here left at junction then continue 3kms to house which is signposted just to the right of the road.

068

Management: Una & Mike Cooper

You may well have heard of the Torcal Natural Park. This is
Andalusia's answer to Capadocia, a huge limestone plateau
which has been gradually weathered into the most
phantasmagorical of shapes by the action of wind and rain. In
its southern lee, just off to one side of one of the province's
quietest roads, this tiny B&B has long been one of my favourite
stopovers in the area, the proof that a good place to stay can
also be a simple place to stay. Mike and Una welcome you with
unaffected hospitality. Their guest house has just three small
bedrooms but these are cosily furnished, sparkling clean and
with comfortable beds: in short, worth every last peseta of their
modest price tag. This is a place where life tends to centre
round the front terrace which has a massive panoramic vista of
the rumpled chains of mountains stretching down towards the
Med. The sunsets here are unbelievable. Una no longer cooks
evening meals but you'll find good food at Bar Durán or
Diego's bar. Should you stay, be sure to visit the nearby El
Chorro gorge.

To see and do: visits to El Chorro gorge and lakes, El Torcal
Natural Park, and the town of Antequera.

LA POSADA DEL TORCAL

Partido de Jeva   **Map: 12**
29230 Villanueva de la Concepción
(Málaga)

Tel: 95 2031177   **Fax:** 95 2031006

e-mail: laposada@mercuryin.es

Web Page: www.andalucia.com/posada-torcal

Closed: December – January.

Bedrooms: 1 Single, 2 "standard" Doubles, 6 "superior" Doubles and 1 Suite.

Prices: Single €96 (16000 Ptas), Standard Double €126 (21000 Ptas), Superior Double €144 (24000 Ptas), Suite €216 (36000 Ptas) + 7% TAX.

Meals: Breakfast included, Lunches from €12 (2000 Ptas) excluding wine, Dinner €29 (4800 Ptas) excluding wine.

Getting there: from Málaga N-331 towards Antequera. Take exit 148 for Casabermeja/Colmenar. In Casabermeja right for Almogía and at junction left at signs for Villanueva de la C. Here up hill then left at junction. After 1.5km right at signs for La Joya/La Higuera. The hotel is to the left of the road after 3km.

069

Management: Karen Ducker

If you like to really get away from it all yet prefer to do so without leaving your creature comforts behind, then the Posada del Torcal will be your type of place. This is one of Andalusía's most highly regarded posadas and one which the Johansen's guide recently voted its "most excellent European country hotel". What I most like about the place are its heart-stopping views and the open-plan bedrooms that have raised corner tubs where you can soak away your troubles without missing a second of the amazing panorama before you. The beds are enormous, the decoration stylishly pick-and-mixes the modern with the traditional, the terracotta tiled floors are underfloor heated and hidden away in a rustic-style cabinet is satellite TV and video. Downstairs is a huge guest lounge and dining room and just beyond a jacuzzi, a gym, an Astroturf tennis court as well as a sauna where you can (try to) pummel away those calories. The Torcal's food is excellent. There are wicked deserts and the wines have been well chosen. A hotel where the accent is very much on the Big Relax.

To see and do: visits to El Torcal Natural Park, El Chorro gorge and lakes, the towns of Antequera and Fuente de la Piedra.

HOTEL LARIOS

Calle Larios 2
29005 Málaga
(Málaga)

Map: 12

Tel: 95 2222200   **Fax:** 95 2222407

e-mail: info@hotel-larios.com

Web Page: www.hotel-larios.com

Closed: Never.

Bedrooms: 3 Doubles, 31 Twins and 6 Suites.

Prices: Double/Twin €98 (16300 Ptas) weekend or €141 (23500 Ptas) weekday, Suite €114 (19000 Ptas) weekend or €177 (29500 Ptas) weekday + 7% TAX.

Meals: Breakfast €9 (1400 Ptas), Lunch/Dinner €30 (5000 Ptas) including wine. Restaurant closed Sundays.

Getting there: from airport towards Málaga centre. Pass El Corte Inglés and continue along broad avenue: La Alameda. At statue (La Estatua del Marqués) left into Calle Larios and hotel is on the left. Staff will help with cases/parking. Or, easier still, park in the Plaza de la Marina and take a taxi to hotel.

070

Management: Pilar Quesada

It's amazing to think how many tourists fly into Málaga airport every year and just how few visit this fascinating city. Part of the reason is that the town has a real dearth of interesting hotels. But if you want a comfortable, safe stay right at the heart of its beautiful old centre, then book a room at the Larios. It is certainly rather different in flavour to most of the other places included within the pages of this guide, a hotel whose focus is predominantly its business clientele and with the corresponding corporate features such as taped music, minibars, safes, satellite tvs, room (and laundry) service and uniformed reception staff. But - hey - we can all enjoy a bit of comfort and the rooms are double-glazed, the beds top-notch and the rooftop bar is a brilliant place for an apéritif with a great view out to the Cathedral, floodlit by night. And all this business-person focus means that the price drops right down at the weekends, the obvious time to plan your visit. Here's a tip to enhance your stay: have a cocktail on the roof, then head out to the Antigua Casa de la Guardía for sherry and seafood.

To see and do: Málaga's monuments and museums, beaches and watersports, Los Montes de Málaga Natural Park.

HOTEL HUMAINA

Parque Natural Montes de Málaga
Ctra Colmenar-Paraje de Cerrado
29013 Málaga
(Málaga)

Map: 12

Tel: 95 2641025   **Fax:** 95 2640115

e-mail: info@hotelhumaina.es

Web Page: www.hotelhumaina.es

Closed: Never.

Bedrooms: 7 Doubles, 4 Twins, 2 Triples and 1 Suite.

Prices: Double/Twin €57 (9500 Ptas), Triple €69 (11500 Ptas), Suite €88 (14600 Ptas) + 7% TAX.

Meals: Breakfast €6 (900 Ptas), Lunch/Dinner €21 (3500 Ptas) including wine.

Getting there: from Málaga N-331 towards Granada then A-355 towards El Colmenar. Just before village turn right on C-345 heading back towards Málaga until you reach crossroads by bar 'Fuente de la Reina'. Just past bar turn right at signs for the hotel and follow 2km of good track to Humaina.

071

Management: Juan María Luna

When the good folk of Málaga need a lung full of fresh mountain air and a leg stretch they head up an extraordinary looping stretch of road to the Montes de Málaga Natural Park. This huge swathe of forest was planted some 60 years back as a water retention measure: previous to this the town had been victim of a number of disastrous floods. Hidden away in a deep valley at the heart of the park, Hotel Humaina is the fruit of the conversion of a former hunting lodge. When the Park was created, so too were new laws limiting the activities of the gun brigade. You couldn't wish for a more bucolic, peaceful location or a better base from which to explore the waymarked paths leading through the forests. The hotel's charming manager Juan María Luna wanted to keep everything as authentic as possible: the furnishing of the dozen bedrooms and cosy guest lounge might be described as elegant rustic, and the same could be said of the restaurant's menu, classical *malagueña* cuisine with the very best ingredients.

To see and do: Los Montes de Málaga Natural Park, Málaga's monuments and museums, the botanical gardens just outside Málaga.

HOSPEDERÍA RETAMAR

Partido Pujeo 30
Riogordo
(Málaga)

Map: 12

Tel: 95 2031225   **Fax:** 95 2031209

Web Page: www.andalucia.com

Closed: Never.

Bedrooms: 11 Doubles (some with a second single bed).

Prices: Double €68–75 (11300–12500 Ptas) including TAX.

Meals: Breakfast €4 (600 Ptas), Lunch/Dinner €15–18 (2500–3000 Ptas) including wine.

Getting there: from Málaga take N-331 northwards then exit for Colmenar on A-355. Bypass Colmenar and after 9km exit for Riogordo and then follow signs north to Retamar along 3kms of track, soon to be tarmacked.

072

Management: José Sánchez Poderera

What is so wonderful about hotel-hopping in Andalusia is not just the places themselves but also the journey there. The wild beauty of the interior of this part of Spain can never fail to move you. Cutting up the long track that leads up from Ríogordo to Retamar you find yourself in a magnificent stretch of wild, limestone mountains, softened occasionally by the olive and almond groves of a sprinkling of isolated farmsteads. The day I first came face to face with Retamar's beguiling palm-graced façade, a Shetland pony ambled across to greet me. This is one of the highest farms in La Axarquía and its hillside perch catches the breezes that blow up off the Med'. It also explains the exceptionally mild climate of the area. Retamar's bedrooms have every mod con (tv, phones and air-conditioning) but what makes the place really special is the fantastic regional cooking. Mention should be made of the aubergines with honey, the snails (when in season) and fantastic cuts of meat served up sizzling on volcanic stones.

To see and do: walking in La Axarquía, day trip to Granada, visits to Antequera and El Torcal Natural Park.

MOLINO DE SANTILLÁN

Ctra. de Macharaviaya km 3
29730 Rincón de Victoria
(Málaga)

Map: 12

Tel: 95 2400949 or 902 120240   **Fax:** 95 2400950

e-mail: msantillan@spa.es

Web Page: www.hotel-msantillan.com

Closed: 10 January – 1 March.

Bedrooms: 4 Doubles and 6 Twins.

Prices: Double/Twin €96–108 (15900–17900 Ptas) + 7% TAX.

Meals: Breakfast €6 (1000 Ptas), Dinner €21 (3500 Ptas) excluding wine.

Getting there: round Málaga on the N-340 towards Motril then exit at km 265 for Macharaviaya. Go up the hill towards Macharaviaya then turn right at sign and follow approx. 1km of track to the hotel.

073

Management: Carlo Marchini

If you want to stay close to the Costa yet sleep deep in the country, then Molino de Santillán would be a perfect choice. This stylishly converted farmhouse is surrounded by groves of avocado and custard fruit and looks south to the glittering Mediterranean, just 3 miles distant. The arches and balconies of this double-storied building have a definite debt to South American hacienda architecture, an impression heightened by an exotic garden of fan palms, agave, honeysuckle and jasmine. You arrive by way of a long, dusty track which is quickly forgotten once you enter the cool, quiet entrance hall. It leads through to the garden where you're greeted by birdsong and that distant sea view. Leading off from this sheltered inner sanctum is the dining room and ten wonderful guest rooms decorated with Ronda-style and antique furniture. Soothing colour schemes are enhanced by stencilling and carefully matched fabrics whilst Casablanca-style fans and mosquito nets heighten that colonial feel. And many of the ingredients of your meal at Santillán come fresh from an extensive, organic vegetable garden.

To see and do: explore the villages of La Axarquía, beaches and watersports, Malaga's museums and monuments.

HOTEL RURAL LOS CARACOLES

Ctra Frigiliana-Torrox km 4.6   **Map: 12**
Lista de Correos de Frigiliana
29788 Frigiliana
(Málaga)

Tel: 95 2030680 or 95 2030609   **Fax:** 95 2030680

e-mail: loscaracoles@ari.es

Web Page: www.hotelloscaracoles.com

Closed: Never.

Bedrooms: 6 Double Snails ('caracoles') and 6 Twins.

Prices: Twin €69 (11500 Ptas), Caracol (snail) €99 (16500 Ptas) + 7% TAX.

Meals: Breakfast €5 (800 Ptas), Lunch/Dinner €21 (3500 Ptas) including wine. Restaurant closed on Mondays and at lunch-time in July and August.

Getting there: from Málaga take the N-340 towards Motril then exit for Frigiliana/Nerja. Then take MA-105 to Frigiliana and here go round bottom of village following signs for Torrox. Los Caracoles is 4.5kms from Frigiliana on the right.

074

Management: Eva León

When did you last sleep in...a snail? This small hotel is without question one of the most unusual places to stay in Andalucía. The position is simply incredible: high above the quiet road which cuts through the foothills of La Axarquía between Torrox and Frigiliana and with the most exhilarating of views out across vine-covered hillsides to Frigiliana and the sea. The extraordinary organic architecture with its sinuous forms and extensive use of mosaic is reminiscent of Gaudí's creations in the Catalan capital, while the earthy colours evoke those of the Maghreb. And it all works incredibly well. Pay the extra and book one of the snails which have been sculpted into the hillside so as to guarantee maximum privacy and the best of views from their private terraces. The architecture of the restaurant is in the same vein and you'll be treated to a culinary as well as an artistic/architectural feast. House specialities include kid, ostrich with walnut sauce, suckling pig and brochette of boar. And there's an interesting vegetarian menu enhanced by the spicy flavours of North Africa.

To see and do: walking, beaches and watersports, visits to Frigiliana, Cómpeta and villages of La Axarquía.

LA POSADA MORISCA

Loma de la Cruz s/n
Ctra de montaña Frigiliana-Torrox
Frigiliana
(Málaga)

Map: 13

Tel: 95 2534151   **Fax:** 95 2534032

e-mail: posada.morisca@terra.es

Closed: 7 - 22 January.

Bedrooms: 2 Doubles and 10 Twins.

Prices: Double/Twin €60–72 (10000–12000 Ptas) + 7% TAX.

Meals: Breakfast included, Lunch/Dinner €15 (2500 Ptas) excluding wine.

Getting there: from Málaga take the N-340 towards Motril then exit for Frigiliana/Nerja. Then take MA-105 to Frigiliana and here go round bottom of village following signs for Torrox. 1.5kms from Frigiliana turn left at sign for hotel: down steep track and then bear left to Posada.

075

Management: Sara Navas Sánchez

As this book goes to press La Posada Morisca is still in its very first year and yet it has already earned an enviable reputation as a wonderful place to eat and to sleep. It is just a few kilometres from Frigiliana, terraced in amongst groves of avocado and mango in one of the most fertile parts of Andalucía's coastal fringe. You couldn't hope to meet with friendlier, kinder hosts than Sara and husband José Luis. The bedrooms that they worked long and hard to create are some of the nicest I've come across: a beautiful mix of rustic Spain (terracotta tiles, latticed wardrobes, wood-burning stoves, handmade tiles from Vélez) with a designer's eye for colour and fabrics. No two are the same and all have panoramic views out to the Mediterranean. And the decoration of the restaurant is just as aesthetically appealing: wafer brick, more terracotta and a bright, ceramic-tiled bar contrasted by floral curtains and soothing, creamy-coloured walls. The cooking is (to quote Sara) 'Mediterranean and innovative' with a fair portion of ingredients grown on the terraced slopes surrounding the farm. Book a night and you'll want to stay a week.

To see and do: caves at Nerja,. Frigiliana, Cómpeta and villages of La Axarquía, beaches and *caletas* (coves) close to Maro.

HOTEL ROMÁNTICO CASA MARO

Calle del Carmen 2   **Map: 13**
29787 Maro
(Málaga)

Tel: 95 2529552 or 95 2529690   **Fax:** 95 2529552

Closed: Never.

e-mail: hotelcasamaro@teleline.es

Bedrooms: 2 Singles and 6 Twins.

Prices: Single €32 (5350 Ptas), Twin €71 (11770 Ptas) including TAX.

Meals: Breakfast €5–10 (795–1695 Ptas), Dinner €45 (7500 Ptas) including wine. Restaurant open from March-October.

Getting there: from Málaga take the N-340 towards Motril then exit for Nerja. Through Nerja to Maro and there take the first right turn as you enter the village. You'll see Casa Maro on the left.

076

Management: Paul W. Ott

As you'd expect given its full name, Casa Maro could be just the place for a romantic break. Maro is a tiny cluster of houses above one of the nicest coves and beaches on this part of the Costa, a short drive from Nerja's famous Balcón de Europa and cave. This sleepy hamlet had a brief moment of glory when a factory was built to extract sugar but soon sank back into obscurity once it closed. You'll have no problems spotting the salmon and peppermint-green walls of Casa Maro whose colour and design had me thinking of villas along the Côte d'Azur. The place would make a great film-set for a Graham Greene novel: the vintage car, the three macaws that officiate over a palm-shaded terrace, potted orchids and aspidistra and views out across groves of avocado and custard-fruit to the sea. The hotel is known (by its mostly German-speaking devotees) for its food. Fresh fish is nearly always on offer as well as plenty of fresh vegetables and interesting sauces. Maro's bedrooms are in a more simple vein. The best look out to sea and the accent is on simple comfort – teamaker and fridge are welcome extras.

To see and do: the Nerja caves, The Balcón de Europa in Nerja, the villages of La Axarquía.

HOTEL PARAÍSO DEL MAR

Calle Prolongación de Carabeo 22   **Map: 13**
29780 Nerja
(Málaga)

Tel: 95 2521621   **Fax:** 95 2522309

e-mail: info@hispanica-colint.es

Web Page: www.hotelparaisodelmar.com

Closed: Mid November – mid December.

Bedrooms: 2 Singles, 4 "normal" Double/Twins, 3 Double/
Twins with jacuzzi and 3 Suites.

Prices: Single €45–69 (7500–11500 Ptas), Double/Twin €51–81
(8500–13500 Ptas), Double with jacuzzi €63–90 (10500–15000
Ptas), Suite €90–120 (15000–19900 Ptas) + 7% TAX.

Meals: Breakfast included, no Lunch/Dinner available: lots of
local and international restaurants within an easy walk of hotel.

Getting there: round Málaga on the N-340 towards Almería
then exit for Nerja. Here follow signs for the Parador: Hotel
Paraíso del Mar is just a few yards away at the edge of the
Balcón de Europa.

077

Management: Enrique Caro Bernal

You'll probably remember two things about Hotel El Paraiso del Mar. One will be the stunning location high above Nerja's long sweep of golden sand. The other will be meeting Enrique Caro Bernal. He is one of a rare breed of hoteliers who, even at the end of the season, is able to greet you with the same warmth and enthusiasm as he would his very first guest. Nowadays visitors will book their holidays a year in advance, yet this is not a man to rest on his laurels: not a year passes without some part of his small hotel being refurbished or refurnished. The hotel has gradually been built up round what was the private villa of an English doctor. Later additions have been added in such a way that you'd have difficulty saying where the original building ends and the new one begins. Several bedrooms and suites have balconies and/or terraces that look out across the cliff-side, terraced gardens to the beach which can be reached by a steep path that drops down from the hotel. Without doubt this is one of the Costa's friendliest small hotels.

To see and do: the Nerja caves, Frigiliana, the villages of La Axarquía.

CÓRDOBA
PROVINCE

Hotels 78 to 85

Córdoba Province

HOSPEDERÍA DE SAN FRANCISCO

Avenida Pío XII 35   **Map: 4**
14700 Palma del Río
(Córdoba)

Tel: 957 710183   **Fax:** 957 645146

e-mail: hospederia@zoom.es

Web Page: www.ibernet.net/lascasas

Closed: Never.

Bedrooms: 14 Doubles and 23 Twins.

Prices: Double/Twin €60–75 (10000–12500 Ptas) + 7% TAX.

Meals: Breakfast €6 (950 Ptas), Lunch/Dinner €18–21 (3000–3500 Ptas) excluding wine.

Getting there: from Córdoba take N-IV towards Sevilla. Exit just before Écija on A-453 to Palma del Río then follow signs to hotel.

078

Management: Jose Alfonso Morilla Espejo

1492 was, as we all know, quite a year for Spain. America was discovered as Columbus sailed west to get east and those pesky Moors were finally sent packing. It was also the year that the 7th Lord of Palma left orders in his Last Testament that a Franciscan monastery should be built. His will was carried out and the monastery he funded served as a retreat for the Brothers until 1985 when it was given a new destiny as one of Andalusia's most charismatic small hotels. The bedrooms, in what were the monk's cells, are wrapped around a series of inter-linked cloisters and patios where ochre, salmon and earth-brown pigments highlight columns and arches in a wonderful symphony of form and colour. The rooms are simply fabulous: their dark wooden furniture, religious prints and original tiled floors hark back to times past, whilst their sparkling bathrooms talk of a different age. So what more could you ask for? A Basque cook? Enter Iñaki Martínez, one of the country's best chefs whose culinary creations, served in the beautiful refectory, will have any gourmet enthusing about this place.

To see and do: the Sierra de Hornachuelos Natural Park, the old town of Palma del Río, Córdoba and Sevilla.

HOTEL ALBUCASIS

Buen Pastor 11   **Map: 4**
14003 Córdoba
(Córdoba)

Tel: 957 478625   **Fax:** 957 478625

Closed: 6 January — 7 February.

Bedrooms: 6 Singles and 9 Doubles.

Prices: Single €36–45 (6000–7500 Ptas), Double €54–69 (9000–11500 Ptas) including TAX.

Meals: Breakfast €5 (850 Ptas), no Lunch/Dinner available: huge choice of restaurants and tapas bars within walking distance.

Getting there: follow signs to Plaza de las Tendillas then take calles Jesús María, Ángel de Saavedra, Blanco Belmonte, Conde y Luque and finally Buen Pastor to the hotel which will be on your right. But much easier to park in any city centre car park and take a taxi to hotel.

079

Management: Alfonso Sales Camacho

Staying somewhere in Córdoba's Jewish quarter has to be first choice if you visit the city, not least because its incredibly narrow streets (laid out with donkeys rather than cars in mind) guarantee a minimum of traffic nuisance. My personal favourite *judería* (Jewish quarter) address is Hotel Albucasis. It is quiet, clean, comfortable, just yards from the synagogue and only a five minute stroll from the Mezquita. You are also just out of the touristy-tack shadow, in a part of town where shopkeepers still manage a smile. The Spanish and Andalusian flags hanging over the entrance will help you spot your hotel. Its portal of dressed stone leads to a pleasant inner courtyard where white, rather rococo wrought-iron garden furniture feels a bit out of synch with the subdued mood of the simple lounge-cum-breakfast room with high French windows to capture the maximum amount of light. It is absolutely spotless and in one corner there's a small bar where you can always get a drink. Bedrooms are simple affairs with marble floors and louvre-doored wardrobes: the nicest is no. 33 which looks out over the rooftops of this enchanting part of Córdoba.

To see and do: the Mezquita and the Jewish quarter, Palace complex of Medina Azahara, walking in the Sierra Morena.

HOTEL NH AMISTAD CÓRDOBA

Plaza de Maimónides 3   **Map: 4**
14004 Córdoba
(Córdoba)

Tel: 957 420335   **Fax:** 957 420365

e-mail: nha-cordoba@nh-hoteles.es

Web Page: www.nh-hoteles.com

Closed: Never.

Bedrooms: 2 Singles, 18 Doubles and 64 Twins.

Prices: Double/Twin €108 (18000 Ptas) + TAX. Add 50% during Feria and Semana Santa.

Meals: Breakfast €10 (1700 Ptas), Lunch/Dinner €30–36 (5000–6000 Ptas) including wine.

Getting there: arriving from the south, cross river and then follow signs for Amistad (with P = Parking sign): the hotel car park is just beyond the Almudaina restaurant (ignore No Entry sign).

080

Management: Francisco Javier Muñoz Valadez

NH Amistad manages to break the mould of the standard "chain" hotel. Although it is much larger than other places in this book, thanks to the friendliness of its staff and the unusual architecture of the place – it embraces a part of the city walls and some rooms are in a separate annex –– it feels both intimate and welcoming. It is also brilliantly central: from here you can walk to the Mezquita through the labyrinthine alleyways of the Jewish quarter in just five minutes. Arriving in its very swish reception area (marble is used as a cooling element throughout the hotel) you at first see little sign of the two 18th century mansions that were renovated to create the hotel. Things get to feel more authentic in the beautiful pebbled inner patio where a fountain and wafer-bricked arches hark back to another age. All bedrooms (the nicest are nos. 201-208) have four-star fittings, snazzy bathrooms, marbled or parquet floors and every conceivable mod con. The buffet breakfast is excellent, too, but I'd skip supper and instead head out to eat in one of the more intimate restaurants of the old Jewish quarter.

To see and do: the Mezquita and the Jewish quarter, Palace complex of Medina Azahara, walking in the Sierra Morena.

HOSTAL SENECA

Conde y Luque 7   **Map: 4**
14003 Córdoba
(Córdoba)

Tel: 957 473234   **Fax:** 957 473234

Closed: Over Christmas period for about 1 month.

Bedrooms: 1 Single, 4 Doubles and 7 Twins. Some rooms share bathroom.

Prices: Single €14–26 (2300–4300 Ptas), Double/Twin with bathroom €33–36 (5500–6000 Ptas), Double/Twin sharing bathroom €26–29 (4300–4800 Ptas) including TAX.

Meals: Breakfast included, no Lunch/Dinner available: huge choice of restaurants and tapas bars within walking distance.

Getting there: Hostal Seneca is in a narrow street just to the north of the Mezquita. Park anywhere in the centre and take a taxi to the hotel – it is difficult to negotiate the very narrow streets of the Jewish quarter.

081

Management: Janine Peignier & María del Pilar Romero

If your travelling on a budget, Hostal Seneca could be a brilliant choice. It certainly isn't grand and if you're one to hanker after bathrobes, satellite tv and minibars then this place won't be for you. This is a typical rambling Córdoban town house with a plant-filled pebbled patio whose striped arches and columns are evocative of those of the Mezquita which is less than 100 yards from the Seneca. This is a very old house: there was a dwelling here during the Moorish period and there's evidence, too, that parts of it date back to Roman times. The house's last big reform was in 1860 and many of the floor tiles, stucco mouldings and the wonderful geometric tiles are from that period. You may not meet with the owners but the friendly, gregarious manager Juan takes good care of his guests, officiating in the tiny wood and tile clad breakfast room-cum-bar. The simple bedrooms follow the twists and turns of the house's original floor plan and so vary in size and configuration. The Seneca gets a mention in all the guides, so you'll need to book ahead.

To see and do: the Mezquita and the Jewish quarter, Palace complex of Medina Azahara, walking in the Sierra Morena.

FINCA BUYTRÓN

Calle Gran Capitán 24   **Map: 4**
14550 Montilla
(Córdoba)

Tel: 957 650152 or 649 577520   **Fax:** 957 650152

Closed: Never.

Bedrooms: 1 Double, 2 Twins and 1 Apartment with 2 twin rooms.

Prices: Double/Twin €60 (10000 Ptas), Apartment for two €72 (12000 Ptas) including TAX.

Meals: Breakfast €3 (500 Ptas), no Lunch/Dinner available: self-catering possible or excellent restaurant a short drive away in Montilla.

Getting there: ring Rafaela who will meet you at Las Camachas restaurant in Montilla and guide you to the farmhouse.

082

Management: Rafaela Mármol Luque

Olive groves and vineyards stretch away from Montilla as far as the eye can see: the town is at the heart of the Cordoban wine producing region where the hardy Pedro Jiménez grape is transformed into a wonderful 'fino' (glossary) style wine. This really feels like that fabled (!) 'real' Andalucía and this old farmhouse would be a fantastic place to stay if you feel happy far away from the tourist-beaten trail. Buytrón was bought 50 years back by Rafaela's grandfather. The area has been farmed since Roman times because of its abundant artesian water and the huge water wheel just beyond the farm house dates back to that time. Rafaela has completely redecorated the place of so many happy childhood memories, managing to conserve all of the house's rustic flavour and authenticity. Warm colour schemes, painted beams, antique furniture, framed cross stitch and old prints create a rather out-of-time feel. The bedrooms are cosy with the accent on simple comfort. At breakfast you can self-cater or be catered-for by Rafaela. Buytrón is a deeply rural, quiet and an enchanting place to really wind down.

To see and do: bodegas of Montilla area, El Convento de Santa Clara., La Casa del Inca Garcillaso de la Vega in Montilla.

HOTEL ZUHAYRA

Calle Mirador 10
14870 Zuheros
(Córdoba)

Map: 5

Tel: 957 694693 or 957 694694   **Fax:** 957 694702

e-mail: zuhayra@teleline.es

Web Page: www.zuheros.com

Closed: Never.

Bedrooms: 4 Doubles and 14 Twins.

Prices: Double/Twin €39–48 (6500-8000 Ptas) + 7% TAX.

Meals: Breakfast included, Lunch/Dinner €10 (1700 Ptas) excluding wine.

Getting there: from Málaga north towards Córdoba on the N-331 to Lucena. As you leave the town turn right at signs for Cabra. There towards Doña Mencía then turn right to Zuheros. Leave your car in car park by castle: the hotel is on the right as you go down Calle Mirador.

083

Management: José & Juan Carlos Ábalos Guerrero

It's puzzling to think why Zuherros isn't better known. It is the most spectacular of villages with whitewashed houses clinging to an outcrop of limestone rock and topped by a high castle. Make the detour and stay at Hotel Zuhayra. From the outside its a rather unexciting edifice but thanks to its prominent location all of its bedrooms look out across the town. They are sparklingly clean with simple pine furniture and the fabrics of bedspreads and curtains have all just been changed. I loved their uncluttered feel and they are very well equipped given their price. On the ground floor there's a large, rather dark bar area. Much nicer in feel is the cosy first floor restaurant where the menu looks to traditional, Andalusian country cuisine. Specialities include wonderful *salmorejo* (a thick gazpacho), *remojón* (made with hake and oranges), aubergines cooked with honey and some interesting salad variations – a rare thing in Andalucía. The two brothers who run the hotel are exceptionally friendly and there are wonderful walks leading out from the village.

To see and do: walking in the Subbética Natural Park, La Cueva de los Murcielagos (the cave of the bats), the local cheese factory.

HOTEL SANTO DOMINGO

El Agua 12   **Map: 5**
14900 Lucena
(Córdoba)

Tel: 957 511100   **Fax:** 957 516295

e-mail: hsantodomingo@husa.es

Web Page: www.husa.es

Closed: Never.

Bedrooms: 4 Singles, 4 Doubles, 20 Twins and 2 Suites.

Prices: Single €58–65 (9700–10700 Ptas), Double/Twin €84–90 (14000–15000 Ptas), Junior Suite €102–105 (17000–17500 Ptas) + 7% TAX.

Meals: Breakfast €4 (650 Ptas), Lunch/Dinner €14 (2250 Ptas) including wine.

Getting there: from Málaga north on the N-331 towards Córdoba. Exit for Lucena and in town centre follow signs to hotel.

084

Management: Juan Manuel Torres Martínez

Lucena is known amongst Andalusians as *la ciudad del mueble* (furniture town) and dozens of unsightly warehouses line the main road past the town. Its old centre has a very different feel. The few tourists who come and all visiting business folk stay at the Santo Domingo. The hotel is the fruit of the complete restoration of an 18th century convent. It turns around an enormous colonnaded patio: a murmuring fountain, marble flags and a vast awning help keep the searing summer heat at bay and when the temperatures drop underfloor heating clocks in. Leading off from the patio is a designerish bar with an attractive ceramic picture of the town's historic buildings. Carpeted corridors lead to the bedrooms that earn four-star status thanks to all the usual gadgetry like mini bars, safes and hairdryers, and they are enhanced by richly coloured fabrics and carpets. The hotel's large vaulted restaurant has a reasonably priced set menu, but if you're a meat-lover try the *buey a la piedra*. And be sure to visit the nearby sanctuary of the Araceli Virgin. From this strategic point you can look out over four of Andalucía's provinces.

To see and do: baroque churches in the old town of Lucena, the Sanctuary of the Araceli Virgin, the Castillo del Moral where Boabdil was held prisoner.

POSADA REAL

Calle Real 14
14800 Priego de Córdoba
(Córdoba)

Map: 5

Tel: 957 541910   **Fax:** 957 540993

e-mail: posadar@arrakis.es

Web Page: www.arrakis.es/~posadar

Closed: Never

Bedrooms: 2 Twins with own bathroom, 1 Twin and 1 Double sharing bathroom and 1 top-floor Flat.

Prices: Double/Twin €42 (7000 Ptas) including TAX.

Meals: Breakfast included, no Lunch/Dinner available: excellent tapas bars and a good restaurant very close to the Posada.

Getting there: from Málaga north on N-331 to Lucena. Just past Lucena take A-336 via Cabra to Priego. Here follow signs "centro ciudad" then 'casco antiguo/histórico'. Park car in the Plaza del Castillo (locals call it the Plaza del Llano). Calle Real leads off this square.

085

Management: Juan López Calvo

Wandering the narrow streets of Priego de Córdoba's old centre feels like returning to another age. In this plexus of narrow alleyways there is no passing traffic to shatter that illusion. And at the heart of what the locals call the *villa* (town), the tiny Posada Real must be first choice if you stay a night here. When Juan López Calvo restored this old house he wanted to make things as authentically *andaluz* as possible. The fruit of his labour is a place to stay that feels far more like a home than a hotel. There are just four bedrooms (plus a flat up under the eaves), each with its own balcony. They have been beautifully decorated by Juan and his family with antiques, old engravings and rich fabrics: bathrooms have hand-painted tiles and "repro" taps. In the warmer months you breakfast in a quiet vine-covered patio where you are treated to freshly squeezed orange juice, local goat's cheese and quince jelly. And just yards away in the adjacent Plaza is the excellent Abravadero restaurant. Don't consider leaving town without visiting the extraordinary Fuente del Rey, another of Andalusia's unsung treasures.

To see and do: the Route of the Baroque of Córdoba including the Fuente del Rey, walking in Subbética Park, the Roman ruins of Almedinilla.

GRANADA
PROVINCE

Hotels 86 to 99

HOTEL LA BOBADILLA

Apartado de Correos 144
18300 Loja
(Granada)

Map: 12

Tel: 958 321861   **Fax:** 958 321810

e-mail: info@la-bobadilla.com

Web Page: www.la-bobadilla.com

Closed: Never.

Bedrooms: 23 Standard and 28 Junior Suites (all twins that can be joined to make king-size doubles) and 9 Suites.

Prices: Standard €222–255 (36900–42400 Ptas), Junior Suite €268–309 (44600–51400 Ptas), Suite for 2 €376–440 (62600–73200 Ptas) + 7% TAX. Prices on request for other Special Suites.

Meals: Breakfast €15 (2500 Ptas), Lunch/Dinner €39 (6500 Ptas) excluding wine.

Getting there: from Málaga take the N-331 then the A-359 towards Granada. Take exit 1 for Salinas then follow signs for Villanueva de Tapia: hotel signposted to the right of the road.

086

Management: Mariano Verdejo Vendrell

The Bobadilla probably offers the most luxurious, most exotic hotel experience in Andalucía, an amazing cocktail of Arabian Nights fantasy with a liberal dash of Hollywood. A 1000 acre estate of holm-oak forest, olive groves and almond groves protect the hotel from the outside world. The place is known by tour operators the world over and especially by the Japanese who are crazy to get married here. They come for the amazing rooms and suites, the excellence of its gourmet cuisine (choose between one of three restaurants) and the enormous range of activities on offer. There are Turkish baths, saunas, jacuzzis, an indoor pool, a gym, archery, riding and tennis. You can shoot, fly over the farm in a light aircraft or a hot air balloon, canoe or kayak, tour the grounds on foot or by 4 wheel drive. You can have a facial or be pummelled by a masseur. The King of Spain has stayed, Placido Domingo too and, wow! – Tom Cruise and Brad Pitt have slept here as well. So get the bank to up your credit card limit and head for Xanadu, right here in the hills of Andalucía.

To see and do: Antequera and the Torcal Natural Park, Archidona, Granada.

PALACIO DE SANTA INÉS

Cuesta de Santa Inés 9, Barrio del Albayzín   **Map: 13**
18010 Granada
(Granada)

Tel: 958 222362   **Fax:** 958 222465

e-mail: sinespal@teleline.es

Web Page: www.lugaresdivinos.com

Closed: Never.

Bedrooms: 4 "standard" Double/Twins, 26 larger Double/
Twins, 3 Suites and the Alhambra Suite.

Prices: Standard Double/Twin €96 (16000 Ptas), Larger Double/
Twin €120 (20000 Ptas), Suite €150 (25000 Ptas), Alhambra Suite
€211 (35000 Ptas) + 7% TAX.

Meals: Breakfast €5 (800 Ptas), no Lunch/Dinner available: huge
choice of restaurants and tapas bars within walking distance.

Getting there: follow signs for centre and then to Plaza Nueva.
Here take the narrow Carrera del Darro and by the first bridge
stop and walk up Cuesta de Santa Inés to hotel: one of their
staff will help you park. But it is much easier to park in any
central car park and then take a taxi to hotel.

087

Management: Nicolás Garrido

The best views of the Alhambra are to be had from the Albaicín hill on the opposite bank of the river Darro. Don't miss climbing up to the San Nicolás mirador. A dozen years ago this was a run-down part of town but it is fast becoming *the* place to live. Just yards from the lively tapas bars lining the course of the river, the Palacio de Santa Inés is one of the city's most attractive small hotels. Like so many of Andalucía's houses, the facade of this 16th century mansion gives little away. But things step up a beat when you pass into the wonderful balustraded, marble-columned patio. The hotel's most memorable features are its renaissance murals, attributed to a pupil of Raphael, and the intricate *múdejar* (post conquest Moorish style architecture) woodwork of some of its ceilings, the most remarkable that of the Alhambra Suite. The bedrooms (several more were being added as we go to press) stylishly marry antiques, modern art and richly coloured kilims and there are always cut flowers to greet you. And some of them look straight out to the Alhambra.

To see and do: the Alhambra of course, the Carthusian monastery of La Cartuja, the Albaicín area.

HOSTAL SUECIA

Calle Molinos   **Map: 13**
Huerta de los Angeles 8
18009 Granada
(Granada)

Tel: 958 225044 or 958 227781   **Fax:** 958 225044

Closed: Never.

Bedrooms: 2 Doubles and 4 Twins with own bathrooms,
1 Double and 3 Twins sharing two bathrooms.

Prices: Double/Twin with bathrom €45 (7500 Ptas), Double/
Twin sharing bathroom €36 (6000 Ptas) including TAX.

Meals: Breakfast €4 (600 Ptas), no Lunch/Dinner available:
huge choice of restaurants and tapas bars a short walk away in
Campo del Príncipe.

Getting there: round Granada following signs for Alhambra on
ringroad. Up hill towards Alhambra then follow signs to
Alhambra Palace hotel. Here go left down Antequerela Baja and
take next sharp right turn to Campo del Príncipe. Cross square,
left into calle Molinos then left again under arch to Suecia.

088

Management: Mari-Carmen Cerdán Mejías

Don't expect the moon if you come and stay at the Suecia. But if you are looking for a quiet, friendly and unassuming place to stay close to the Alhambra that won't cost an arm or a leg, then you're bound to enjoy this modest *hostal*. The position is wonderful, right at the end of a quiet cul-de-sac and just a five minute stroll from the Campo del Príncipe, a lively square which has dozens of bars and restaurants. The house's facade strikes a merry note with balconied windows picked out by broad bands of ochre and its small front garden awash in greenery. Can you really be in a city centre? One of the hotel's long-serving staff greets you and hands over your key. The Suecia's bedrooms are up on the first and second floor and are simply decorated with wooden furniture, sugary prints and light green curtains and bedspreads. Nothing fancy but perfectly adequate. Breakfasts are served in the small, second floor dining room that looks out onto a roof top terrace. From here there are wonderful views of the Alhambra hill – without doubt the hotel's most special feature.

To see and do: the Alhambra of course, the Carthusian monastery of La Cartuja, the Albaicín area.

HOTEL CARMEN DE SANTA INÉS

Placeta de Porras 7
San Juan de los Reyes 15
18010 Granada
(Granada)

Map: 13

Tel: 958 226380   **Fax:** 958 224404

e-mail: sinescar@teleline.es

Web Page: www.madeinspain.net/hotelesgranada/carmen

Closed: Never.

Bedrooms: 4 Doubles, 1 Twin, 3 Suites with small lounge and 1 Suite with larger lounge.

Prices: Double/Twin €96 (16000 Ptas), Suite (with small lounge) €120 (20000 Ptas), Suite (with larger lounge) €180 (30000 Ptas) + 7% TAX.

Meals: Breakfast €5 (800 Ptas), no Lunch/Dinner available: huge choice of restaurants and tapas bars within walking distance.

Getting there: don't try driving here! It is best to park in Parking San Agustín (or any other city centre car park) and take a taxi to the hotel: the narrow streets of the Albaicín are a nightmare to negotiate.

089

Management: Nicolás Garrido

Granada's *carmens* are amongst Andalucía's most attractive architectural creations. The term is used to describe a town house with a walled garden. They nearly always have an intimate, hidden-world feel about them and many of those on Granada's Albaicín hill first saw the light during Moorish times. The Carmen de Santa Inés has a rather grander air than most of them after an extensive reform in the 17th century. The building's soul is its tiny patio-courtyard where the murmur of a simple marble fountain is the first sound to greet you when you come in from the Albaicín's narrow streets. A heavy wooden door leads out to the garden where another fountain echoes the water music and where the view of the Alhambra is a heady enticement to sit and while away an afternoon. Nicolás Garrido has worked wonders with the Carmen's decoration which, like the nearby Palacio de Santa Inés, is an attractive pot pourri of antiques, modern art and warm colour washes. Suites are worth the extra pesetas (the normal doubles are rather small) and the Mirador is the best one with its view across to the Alhambra.

To see and do: the Alhambra of course, the Carthusian monastery of La Cartuja, the Albaicín area.

HOTEL AMERICA

Real de La Alhambra 53   **Map: 13**
18009 Granada
(Granada)

Tel: 958 227471   **Fax:** 958 227470

e-mail: hamerica@moebius.es

Web Page: www.hamerica.com

Closed: Never.

Bedrooms: 4 Singles, 6 Doubles and 5 Twins.

Prices: Single   61–84 (10175–14000 Ptas), Double/Twin   90
(15000 Ptas) including TAX.

Meals: Breakfast   6 (1000 Ptas), simple Lunches/Dinners   15
(2500 Ptas) excluding wine.

Getting there: round Granada following signs for Alhambra
on the 'Ronda Sur' ringroad. Go up the hill towards the
Alhambra then follow signs to hotel making sure to keep to the
left so as not to enter car parks. Leave baggage at hotel and
then leave car in one of the Alhambra car parks.

090

Management: Maribel Alconchel

For years and years Hotel America has been one of the very best places to stay in Granada. There's only one problem. Unless you book weeks ahead the chances are that it will be full. The reason for its popularity is not only that it is an immensely attractive hotel just yards from the Alhambra. It is also because of the good, old-fashioned hospitality of the Alonchel family. Three generations of them have managed the America since it opened it doors in 1936. Previous to that it had been the summer residence of a well-to-do Duchess. Guests invariably gravitate towards a plant-filled courtyard which doubles as the hotel's restaurant. Here sparrows hop between ceramic-topped tables and a Virginia creeper and rambling ivy help keep the sun at bay. It can get busy at lunchtime and is best enjoyed later in the day when the coach parties are heading back down the hill. I would try to book a bedroom on the top floor (nos 212 or 214) which have recently been completely redecorated in a warm (sponged) ochre tones and which feel as welcoming as the rest of the hotel.

To see and do: the Alhambra of course, the Carthusian monastery of La Cartuja, the Albaicín area.

HOTEL CASA MORISCA

Cuesta de la Victoria 9   **Map: 13**
18010 Granada
(Granada)

Tel: 958 221100   **Fax:** 958 215796

e-mail: info@casamorisca.com

Web Page: www.hotelcasamorisca.com

Closed: Never.

Bedrooms: 3 Doubles, 8 Twins and 2 Suites.

Prices: Double/Twin €132 (22000 Ptas), Suites €156–180 (26000–30000 Ptas) + 7% TAX.

Meals: Breakfast €7 (1200 Ptas), no Lunch/Dinner available: huge choice of restaurants and tapas bars within walking distance.

Getting there: from the Plaza Nueva follow the Acera del Darro almost to the end (the Alhambra will be to your right) and the Cuesta de La Victoria is last-but-one turning to the left. Or park anywhere in centre and take taxi to hotel.

091

Management: María Jesús Candenas & Carlos Sánchez

The Casa Morisca is still in it first year as this book goes to press, the latest of the Albaicín's mansion houses to have been transformed into a charming small hotel. This is a very old house. The owners have documents tracing its origins back to the end of the 15th century. As its name suggests, the architecture of the house is that beloved of the Moors, a style that continued to be prevalent long after their expulsion. Here are wafer-brick columns, delicate keyhole arches, polychromatic tiles with Arabic calligraphy and the most amazing of *mudéjar* (post conquest Moorish syle of architecture) wooden ceilings. This is the perfect place to stay to prolong that Alhambra moment, and from many of the fourteen bedrooms you look straight out to the Comares tower. All have been magnificently decorated. There are intricate Alhambra-style mouldings, bright kilims, pastel colours and fabulous bathrooms. The lighting is subtle, the beds superb and the place is surprisingly quiet given the city centre location. You breakfast in a barrel-vaulted dining room with the murmur of the courtyard fountain to accompany your meal.

To see and do: the Alhambra of course, the Carthusian monastery of La Cartuja, the Albaicín area.

EL CORTIJO DEL PINO

Fernán Nuñez 2   **Map: 13**
La Loma
18659 Albuñuelas
(Granada)

Tel: 958 776257 or 607 523767   **Fax:** 958 776257

Closed: Never.

Bedrooms: 5 Double/Twins and 1 Apartment.

Prices: Double/Twin €60 (10000 Ptas) including TAX.

Meals: Breakfast included, Dinner €12 (2000 Ptas) excluding wine.

Getting there: from Málaga to Granada (N-331, NA-359 then A-92). Just before arriving in Granada branch onto motorway towards Motril then take exit for Albuñuelas. Here as you arrive in village turn right by a bus stop. A steep road leads you up to El Cortijo del Pino.

092

Management: Antonia Ruano & James Connel

You can spot the massive Aleppo pine tree that towers above Cortijo del Pino and gives the house its names from miles away. It stands guardian to the old farmhouse that this Anglo-Spanish couple have recently turned into one of Andalusia's most attractive small B&Bs. They run it in the very best tradition of *mi casa es tu casa* (my home is your home). James is an artist and sometimes gives courses at the house (details on request). There would be plenty to inspire you whether you were painting a still life or a landscape. Every corner of this house has been decorated and arranged with an artist's sensitivity and the views out across the wooded valley to Albuñuelas are magnificent. You won't want for space in the bedrooms which have been beautifully decorated by Antonia with the family antiques, huge beds, beautiful tiles, hand-embroidered curtains and of course James' paintings. When I stayed at El Pino I awoke to the sound of birdsong and the chiming of the church bells across the valley. And I have wonderful memories of a delicious dinner in the very best of company.

To see and do: the Lecrín Valley, the villages of La Alpujarra, Granada and its Alhambra.

HOTEL ALBERGUE DE MECINA

Calle La Fuente s/n
18416 Mecina Fondales
(Granada)

Map: 14

Tel: 958 766241 or 958 766241   **Fax:** 958 766255

e-mail: alpujarr@ctv.es

Web Page: www.ctv.es/alpujarr

Closed: Never.

Bedrooms: 18 large rooms (with a double and 2 single beds) and 3 smaller doubles.

Prices: Double €53 (8850 Ptas), Triple use €69 (11500 Ptas) and Quadruple use €81 (13500 Ptas) + 7%TAX.

Meals: Breakfast €5 (850 Ptas), Lunch/Dinner €12 (2000 Ptas) excluding wine.

Getting there: from Granada take new motorway south towards Motril then exit on the C-333 through Lanjarón. As you reach Órgiva take the road via Pampaneira towards Pitres. 1km before Pitres turn right down hill to Mecina. The hotel is at top the of the village.

093

Management: Encarna Ortega

More and more people are visiting the Alpujarras, especially at the weekends, and tourist shops now line the streets of places like Pampaneira and Trevélez. You'll escape the crowds at the Albergue de Mecina which is in one of the area's lesser known villages (it's been open for several years but only after recent change of management has it become a place to recommend). You'll probably be greeted in reception by the charming, quiet-mannered Encarna Ortega. Be sure to ask her for one of the rooms at the rear of the building which have views out across the steep-sided *barranco* (gorge) of the River Trevélez. Most of them are massive and have been redecorated and refurnished with bright fabrics, dark wooden bedside tables and dressers and pictures with a floral theme. The hotel's best feature is its dining room which is decorated in a more rustic style than the bedrooms. Dark beams support a traditional dark slate roof, tables are prettily laid with pink cloths and cut flowers and the food is excellent – all the typical dishes of the Alpujarras and, as we went to press, an organic vegetable garden was being planted.

To see and do: walking, the Roman bridge in Fondales, the Buddhist monastery above Pampaneira.

SIERRA Y MAR

Calle Albaycín 16   **Map: 14**
18416 Ferreirola
(Granada)

Tel: 958 766171   **Fax:** 958 857367

e-mail: reservas@sierraymar.com

Web Page: www.sierraymar.com

Closed: January.

Bedrooms: 2 Singles, 4 Doubles and 3 Twins.

Prices: Single €27 (4500 Ptas), Double/Twin €42 (7000 Ptas) including TAX.

Meals: Breakfast 3 (500 Ptas), no Lunch/Dinner available: restaurant a ten minute walk from Sierra y Mar in Fondales.

Getting there: from Granada take motorway south towards Motril then exit on the C-333 via Lanjarón to Órgiva. Just before you enter Órgiva branch left on GR-421. Go through Pampaneira and just before Pitres turn right to Mecina. Through village to Ferreirola: park in square and walk final 100 yards to house.

094

Management: Inger Norgaard & Giuseppe Heiss

Jose and Inge have run this simple B&B for several years and were amongst the very first foreigners to settle in this part of the Alpujarra. They chose the tiniest of hamlets, Ferreirola, where donkeys still outnumbered cars and where there would be no chance of being disturbed by passing traffic. The road ends in the square and you walk the final fifty yards to Sierra y Mar's cheerful blue entrance. It leads to a shady, walled garden where time seems to slow down a pace or two. The emphasis here is on what is simple, home-spun, wholesome and authentic. Bedrooms have none of those chain-hotel extras but are all clean, comfortable and quiet. Most are in the main house where there is a guest lounge with masses of documentation on walking. Groups from the UK use the place as a a base and few people know the mountains round here like José. There's a wonderful walk straight out from the house and although only breakfast is available just ten minute's walk from the house is one of the area's most characterful restaurants.

To see and do: walking and riding, the Roman bridge in Fondales, the nearby villages of Las Alpujarras.

ALQUERÍA DE MORAYMA

A-348 Cádiar-Torvizcón   **Map: 14**
18440 Cádiar
(Granada)

Tel: 958 343221 or 958 343303   **Fax:** 958 343221

e-mail: morayma@arrakis.es

Web Page: www.alqueriademorayma.com

Closed: Never.

Bedrooms: 8 Double/Twins and 5 Houses.

Prices: Double/Twin €45 (7500 Ptas), House for two €57 (9500 Ptas), House for four €75 (12500 Ptas) excluding TAX.

Meals: Breakfast €3 (500 Ptas), Lunch/Dinner €10 (1600 Ptas) including wine.

Getting there: from Granada take the N-323 south towards Motril then exit on the A-348 to Lanjarón. Here continue to Órgiva and Torvizcón towards Cádiar. The Alquería de Morayma is 2km before Cádiar to the left of the road.

095

Management: Mariano Cruz Fajardo

The Alquería de Morayma lies just east of the deep *barranco* (gorge) that author Chris Stewart recently put on the map in his best-selling "Driving Over Lemons". This is fantastic walking country and the long distance foot-path that winds its way across the Alpujarra passes just yards from Morayma. Mariano Cruz wanted to create something more than a place to sleep and eat at La Alquería. He wants guests to actually immerse themselves in the traditional way of life of the area. So you can join in with the harvest and the milling of the farm's olives, you can help to make goat's cheese, bring in the grapes or even take part in the winter *matanza* (the slaughter and preparation of a pig). This is a place where you'd want to spend several nights. The rooms and houses recreate the feel of one of the region's villages – an organic, inter-linked whole that centres round the bar and restaurant. Rooms have been conceived as comfortable living spaces as well as an ethnographical testament to all that is local. And the restaurant's menu, as you'd expect, offers the same time-tried recipes that you might find in any traditional Alpujarran home.

To see and do: walking and horse-riding, visit to a *secadero* where cured hams are prepared.

HOTEL LA FRAGUA

Calle San Antonio 4   **Map: 14**
18417 Trevélez
(Granada)

Tel: 958 858626 or 958 858573   **Fax:** 958 858614

e-mail: fragua@navegalia.com

Closed: 10 January - 10 February.

Bedrooms: 3 Singles, 3 Doubles and 8 Twins.

Prices: Single €19 (3200 Ptas), Double/Twin €30 (5000 Ptas) +
7% TAX.

Meals: Breakfast €2 (350 Ptas), Lunch/Dinner €9 (1500 Ptas)
including wine.

Getting there: from Granada take new motorway south towards
Motril then exit on the C-333. Go through Lanjarón and just
before Órgiva turn left toTrevélez. Here go steeply up hill to the
'barrio medio' and park near to La Plaza de las Pulgas. La
Fragua is next to the *ayuntamiento* (town hall).

096

Management: Antonio & Miguel Espinosa

Trevélez is one of the better-known villages in la Alpujarra. A lot of people come here to walk. From here you can climb the Sierra Nevada's highest peak, the Mulhacén (you'll be starting at a height of nearly 1500m!) and the GR-7 long distance footpath loops past the village. La Fragua is one of the village's highest buildings, and from its rooftop terrace there is an amazing vista of the river valley and the distant Contraviesa sierra. The bedrooms – as you'd expect given their paltry price tag – are nothing grand but they are quiet, clean and those on the first floor have balconies facing out onto the (pedestrianised) street. Breakfasts and other meals are served at the sister restaurant of the same name, just 50 yards down the street. It has a cosy pine-clad dining room which has been hoisted above the bar with windows to three sides that catch that same wonderful view out across the village. La Fragua's menu focuses on things traditional. Try the spicy lamb (*cordero a la moruña*), the partridge (*perdíz del cura a la antigua*) or the generously priced set menu.

To see and do: visit to a *secadero* where cured hams are prepared, trout-fishing in the Río Trevélez (early May to early September) and walking.

HOTEL LOS BÉRCHULES

Ctra de Bérchules 20
18451 Bérchules
(Granada)

Map: 14

Tel: 958 852530   **Fax:** 958 769000

e-mail: hot.berchules@interbook.net

Web Page: www.berchules.com

Closed: Never.

Bedrooms: 10 Twins.

Prices: Twin €36 (6000 Ptas) including TAX.

Meals: Breakfast €3 (500 Ptas), Lunch €6 (1000 Ptas) including wine, Dinner €15 (2500 Ptas) including wine.

Getting there: from Málaga take the N-340 to Motril. Just past Motril turn left to Albuñol and shortly after the village turn right on GR-433 to Cadiar. Here follow signs for Mecina then turn left to Bérchules. The hotel is at the bottom of the village on the left.

097

Management: Alejandro Tamborero

Bérchules is one of the lesser known villages of the Alpujarras. Surrounded by chestnut forests and terraces, irrigated by fast-flowing water channels, its cool mountain air means that this is perfect ham-curing terrain. The hiking round here is magnificent (the GR-7 paths loops through the village) and Hotel Los Bérchules would be great first choice of hotel for walkers – and non-walkers, too. Alejandro and his English mother Wendy greet their guests in a genuine, unaffected manner. There's nothing grand about their simple triple-storied hotel but the bedrooms are all that you need and more. They are all twin-bedded with pine furniture and French windows that lead out to terraces overlooking the valley. Bright, alpujarra-weave blankets and curtains add a welcome splash of colour. The same fabric brightens the cosy bar-cum-lounge on the ground floor where there's a collection of books on the area and a few novels, and across the way is a similarly snug-feeling dining room. The food is good, the set menu excellent value and Wendy is used to vegetarians and their ways. Her wines are also very honestly priced.

To see and do: visit to a *secadero* where cured hams are prepared, walking, and horse-riding.

CASA RURAL LAS CHIMENEAS

Calle Amargura 6　　　　　　　　　**Map: 14**
18493 Mairena
(Granada)

Tel: 958 760352　**Fax:** 958 760004

e-mail: dillsley@moebius.es

Web Page: www.moebius.es/contourlines

Closed: Never.

Bedrooms: 2 Doubles and 1 Twin in main house, 2 Studio-Apartments and 1 house with 2 Doubles.

Prices: Double/Twin/Apartment €48–60 (8000–10000 Ptas) including TAX.

Meals: Breakfast incl. in Double/Twin price but not apartment price, Packed Lunches €5 (750 Ptas), Dinner €15 (2500 Ptas) excluding wine.

Getting there: from Granada A-92 east towards Almería. After passing Guadix take the exit for La Calahorra then go over pass of 'El Puerto de la Ragua' to Laroles. Here right to Mairena. Take the second right into the village and park in the square. Las Chimeneas is just 30m off the south-east corner of square.

098

Management: Emma & David Illsley

David and Emma lived and worked in many different parts of Europe before heading for La Alpujarra, inspired in part by English author Gerald Brennan's writings about the area. They arrived in the right place at just the right time. An architect who had completely restored this old village house had decided to move on. It's easy to see why they fell in love with the house and the village. Mairena is beyond the day-trippers shadow at the eastern end of the Alpujarra, a quiet, friendly village "where mules still outnumber cars". The village looks out across deep *barrancos* (gorges) to the distant Contraviesa mountains. The atmosphere that the whole house seems to breathe is one of wholesome, uncluttered simplicity. There is a high-ceilinged guest lounge/diner with a hearth, books, rocking chairs and light streaming in from its south-facing windows. The bedrooms are every bit as attractive and most are large, some have terraces and all have wonderful old floors and antique furniture. Many of the guests at Las Chimeneas come to explore the mountains surrounding the village and the Illsleys know all of its loveliest pathways.

To see and do: walking (high peaks of 8000 feet easily accessible), horse-riding, visits to other little-known villages such as Júbar.

REFUGIO DE NEVADA

Ctra de Mairena   **Map: 14**
18493 Laroles
(Granada)

Tel: 958 760320 or 958 760304   **Fax:** 958 760338

e-mail: alpujarr@ctv.es

Web Page: www.ctv.es/alpujarr

Closed: Never.

Bedrooms: 2 Doubles, 3 Twins and 7 Studios.

Prices: Double/Twin €41 (6800 Ptas), Studio €53 (8750 Ptas) + 7%TAX.

Meals: Breakfast €4 (650 Ptas), Lunch/Dinner €9 (1500 Ptas) including wine.

Getting there: from Granada A-92 eastwards. Shortly past Guadix turn right and go over the high "El Puerto de La Ragua" pass and continue to Laroles. The hotel is on the right as you enter the village.

099

Management: Victor Fernández Garcés

Laroles lies at the very eastern end of the Alpujarra. You drop
down to the village after following the snaking road that leads
up and over the spectacular pass of La Ragua. There is
wonderful walking here and cross-country skiing when the
snows are down. Another good reason for visiting the area is to
stay at the Refugio de Nevada. This immensely attractive small
hotel is less than a decade old but looks much older thanks to
its architect having faithfully followed the dictates of the local
architectural lore. Its wooden doors, beams and balconies, slate
walls and flat roofs of local *pizarra* slate all feel authentically
alpajarreño. And you know that you've come to the right place
when you're greeted by the warm-hearted, gregarious Eloisa
who officiates in the Refugio's cosy little restaurant. The set
menu (*genuine comida casera*) changes daily with a lot of the
ingredients fresh from husband Manolo's vegetable patch. And
the bedrooms are just as snug and welcoming as the rest of the
hotel: the studios have their own small lounge.

To see and do: horse-riding, walking, visits to other villages of
the Alpujarras.

JAÉN
PROVINCE

Hotels 100 to 104

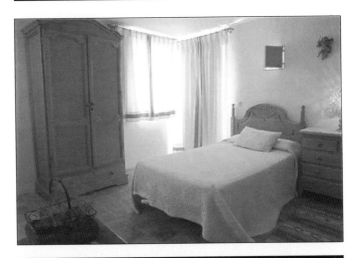

HOSPEDERÍA FUENTENUEVA

Paseo Arca del Agua s/n
23440 Baeza
(Jaén)

Map: 6

Tel: 953 743100   **Fax:** 953 743200

e-mail: fuentenueva@fuentenueva.com

Web Page: www.fuentenueva.com

Closed: Never.

Bedrooms: 3 Doubles and 9 Twins

Prices: Double/Twin €62–63 (10300–10500 Ptas) + 7% TAX.

Meals: Breakfast included, Lunch/Dinner €17 (2800 Ptas) including wine.

Getting there: from Granada take the N-323 north towards Madrid/Jaén. Just before Jaén branch right on the N-321 to Baeza. Exit for Baeza, head all the way through the town centre (where you will pick up signs for Úbeda). The hotel is on the left as you leave the town.

100

Management: Juan Ramón Orcera

Be honest. When was the last time that you went to prison? There can be few places quite as special as Fuentenueva for "doing time". This small hotel occupies, as you'll have guessed, what once was the town prison for women. It was given a new destiny after the local council gave it a thorough face-lift and entrusted its management to a team of five young folk from the town. Thanks to buckets of youthful enthusiasm and creativity, they already have helped to create a truly original place to stay. Downstairs is an airy entrance hall with a ceramic tiled fountain and a bar and restaurant to either side. All of it is decorated in pastel colours and there is modern art hung in every last corner – Fuentenueva doubles as a gallery where local artists can exhibit their work. The same love of colour is evident in the bedrooms which have brightwashes, stencilling and ragged-and-sponged paint finishes. Gaily coloured fabrics add a further dash of razzmatazz. The Hospedería is a hotel with a light heart and beautiful,Rrenaissance Baeza is right on your doorstep.

To see and do: Baeza and its Renaissance architecture, Úbeda and its Renaissance architecture, the Cazorla Natural Park.

MARÍA DE MOLINA

Plaza del Ayuntamiento
23400 Úbeda
(Jaén)

Map: 6

Tel: 953 795356   **Fax:** 953 793694

e-mail: hotelmm@hotel-maria-de-molina.com

Web Page: www.hotel-maria-de-molina.com

Closed: 15 July - 15 August.

Bedrooms: 2 Singles, 6 Doubles and 10 Twins.

Prices: Single €42–60 (7000-10000 Ptas), Standard Double/Twin €66–90 (11000–15000 Ptas), Special Double/Twin €90–120 (15000-20000 Ptas) + 7% TAX.

Meals: Breakfast included, Lunch/Dinner €15 (2500 Ptas) excluding wine.

Getting there: from Granada take the N-323 north towards Madrid/Jaén. Just before Jaén branch right on the N-321 to Úbeda then follow signs for 'Casco Antiguo'. The hotel is next door to the *ayuntamiento* (town hall), signposted as you reach the centre.

101

Management: Juan Navarro López

Nothing quite prepares you for the magnificence of Úbeda. The town, adrift in a vast ocean of olive groves, is absolutely bursting with stunning Renaissance architecture. All of this grandeur dates from a time when the town's merchants grew rich from the textiles that they traded throughout Europe. Times changed and the town became a sleepy backwater. To wander through its streets by night feels like stepping back into a different age. But María de Molina happily spans the gulf between time past and present. This is the only three-story *palacete* (grand mansion house) in town and the building's joy is its beautifully proportioned courtyard with a splendid double tier of marble columns. In other parts of the hote, it's hard to believe that you are really sleeping in a 400-year old building. The bedrooms have the comfort, feel and fittings of a five star hotel and the two dining rooms retain few of their original features. What makes the place memorable is the friendliness of the staff, its excellent food and, of course, the joy of visiting this wonderful old town.

To see and do: Úbeda and its Renaissance architecture, Baeza and its Renaissance architecture, the Cazorla Natural Park.

MOLINO LA FARRAGA

Calle Camino de la Hoz s/n, Apartado de Correos 1   **Map: 6**
23470 Cazorla
(Jaén)

Tel: 953 721249 or 610 737661   **Fax:** 953 721249

e-mail: farraga@teleline.es

Web Page: www.molinolafarraga.com

Closed: 15 December - 15 January.

Bedrooms: 1 Single, 3 Doubles, 3 Twins and 1 Suite.

Prices: Single €32 (5300 Ptas), Double/Twin €55 (9100 Ptas),
Suite €65 (10700 Ptas) including TAX.

Meals: Breakfast included, Picnic Lunches €5 (800 Ptas), Dinner
€9 (1500 Ptas) including wine. Prior reservation essential.

Getting there: in Cazorla follow signs for Ruinas de Santa
María (very narrow streets!) At far side of the Plaza de Santa
María take road leading between ruined church and "Cueva"
restaurant, signposted Castillo. Park on left by sign for La
Farraga then cross bridge and continue on foot for 100m to La
Farraga.

102

Management: Nieves Santana Martín

You reach Cazorla by way of a vast sea of olive groves. After this seemingly endless monoculture, it comes as a relief to see a rugged mountain crest rising up in the distance. And standing sentinel to the sierra you catch sight of Cazorla, a white town that clings to its steep eastern flank. The prettiest part of the town is a delightful small square by the ruined church of Santa María and just up the valley from here the old mill house of La Farraga must surely be one of the very nicest places to stay in Andalucía. You abandon your car 100 yards before La Farraga, cross a small bridge and then follow a riverside path to the mill. Its wonderfully verdant garden is criss-crossed by water channels, birds sing amongst the foliage and Nieves greets you with the kindest of smiles. Inside the mill house the feel is one of simple, unaffected comfort and well-being. Rooms vary in dimensions, all are beautifully decorated and feel fresh, airy and peaceful. Nieves will prepare you a picnic lunch if you're here to walk and her breakfasts and dinners are as appetising as the house itself.

To see and do: Parque Natural de Cazorla, the old town of Cazorla, Úbeda and Baeza and their Renaissance architecture.

HOTEL LA FINCA MERCEDES

Ctra de la Sierra km 1   **Map: 6**
23476 La Iruela
(Jaén)

Tel: 953 721087   **Fax:** 953 720624

Closed: Never.

Bedrooms: 3 Doubles, 4 Twins and 2 Triples.

Prices: Double/Twin €30–33 (5000-5500 Ptas).

Meals: Breakfast €3 (450 Ptas), Lunch/Dinner €9 (1400 Ptas) excluding wine.

Getting there: from Úbeda take the N-322 towards Albacete then branch onto A-315 then A-319 to Cazorla. Here continue up to large square at centre of town and turn left at signs for La Iruela. Stay on this road and you pass just beneath La Iruela. La Finca Mercedes is on the left after about 1km.

103

Management: Mercedes Castillo

If you're looking for a cheap and cheerful place to lay your head when visiting the wonderful Cazorla Park, you couldn't do better than book a night or two at this modest hotel. The life and soul of the place is Mercedes Castillo. Its fitting that the hotel should have been named after her. I stayed several nights here when researching a walking guide and was made to feel a part of the family. Things are on a human scale here. The bedrooms are average-sized, decorated with simple pine furniture and the nicest look out across the vast expense of olive groves that lies to the east of Cazorla. They are quiet, comfortable and very warm in the winter months (this part of Andalucía can get very cold). The dining room has the same really inviting, snug feel about it. A fire burns in the hearth in the colder months and there are paintings of Cazorla and the sea interspersed with a collection of hunting trophies. Simple, regional dishes are on the menu and Mercedes' two daughters, rather quieter than Mum, will often be there to serve you.

To see and do: Parque Natural de Cazorla, the old town of Cazorla, Úbeda and Baeza and their Renaissance architecture.

LA MESA SEGUREÑA

Calle Postigo 2   **Map: 7**
23379 Segura de la Sierra
(Jaén)

Tel: 953 482101 or 953 503370

Fax: 953 482101 or 953 503370

Closed: 8 - 31 January.

Bedrooms: 2 two room Apartments (further rooms are currently under construction near to La Mesa S.)

Prices: Apartment for two €48 (8000 Ptas), Apartment for four €72 (12000 Ptas) including TAX.

Meals: Breakfast provided on first day, Lunch/Dinner €18 (3000 Ptas) including wine. Restaurant closed Sunday and Monday night.

Getting there: from Jaén take the A-316 and then the N-322 towards Albacete. Exit for Puente de Génave and then follow A-317 via La Puerta de Segura to Orcera and then Segura. La Mesa Segureña is signposted as you reach the village centre.

104

Management: Ana María Solares & Francisco Jiménez Aldehuela

You see Segura de la Sierra from miles away. This is the Cazorla Park's most spectacular village, built on a rocky crag that rises high above the olive groves and crowned by its lofty castle. Surprisingly few people visit this part of the Park, yet this beautiful village and the walking round here (see Santana's book "Walking in Andalucía") make a visit a double treat. Be sure to stay at La Mesa Segureña. As the name suggests, this place has a distinct culinary focus. Ana María is an artist and she worked wonders when decorating the restaurant and apartments. The general theme is rustic but with a really jazzy feel thanks to her use of warm colours (mostly greens and salmon), the abundance of posters and paintings (many her own creations) and her desire that everything should feel "just so". Given the standard of comfort, the apartments are very reasonably priced, and even more so for a family of four. The restaurant offers regional food with a dash of creativity and there is a really good selection of wine on offer.

To see and do: the castle of Segura de la Sierra, walking in the Cazorla Natural Park, visit to one of the only square bullrings in Spain.

ALMERÍA
PROVINCE

Hotels 105 to 111

HOSTAL ELDORADO

Ctra Genoveses   **Map: 15**
4118 San José
(Almería)

Tel: 950 380118 or 950 380269   **Fax:** 950 380246

e-mail: eldoradosanjose@wanadoo.es

Closed: Never.

Bedrooms: 12 Doubles and 3 Twins.

Prices: Double/Twin €36–54 (6000–9000 Ptas) including TAX.

Meals: Breakfast €3 (500 Ptas), Lunch (snacks), Dinner €21 (3500 Ptas) including wine. Restaurant closed on Mondays in Low Season.

Getting there: from N-344 take exit 479 towards Níjar/San Isidro then follow signs to San José. Signposted to right as you enter village: or follow "Playas" and you'll see the hostal on the right.

105

Management: Alain Patrick

San José has seen considerable change over the past decade. It has become a favourite destination of both Spaniards and foreigners and several tiers of holiday apartments now stretch back from its arc of sandy beach. But it is still worth a visit. The village retains considerable charm, you are close to two of the best beaches in Spain and there are wonderful walks along the coast of the Cabo de Gata Natural Park. This French owned hotel is by far the nicest place to stay in the village. Although it stands well back from the beach, you still catch a glimpse of the sea from this modern, two storey building. All of its bedrooms (a further 10 were being built as we went to press) have their own terraces, and there is an almost Zen feel to them. They are clean, light and colourful, and the yellow curtains, blue window frames and the deep rust brown of the floor tiles work really well together. Being French owned, you would expect the food to be good – and it certainly is, mixing Spanish with international dishes. The pastry is superb (try the salmon and prawn in "thousand leaf" pastry), the fish is fresh and the service fast and friendly.

To see and do: the beaches of Monsúl and Los Genoveses, the mining village of Rodalquilar, the village and beach of Las Negras.

HOSTAL FAMILY

Calle La Lomilla s/n   **Map: 15**
4149 Agua Amarga
(Almería)

Tel: 950 138014   **Fax:** 950 138070

e-mail: riovall@teleline.es

Closed: Never.

Bedrooms: 1 Double, 7 Twins and 1 Quadruple.

Prices: Double/Twin €60–72 (10000–12000 Ptas), Quadruple €72–96 (12000–16000 Ptas) including TAX.

Meals: Breakfast included, Lunch (weekends only) €12 (2000 Ptas) including wine, Dinner €12 (2000 Ptas) including wine.

Getting there: from N-344 take exit 494 signposted Venta del Pobre/Carboneras. Continue towards Carboneras and then turn right to Agua Amarga. Hostal Family signposted to right as you enter the village.

106

Management: Michèle, Marcos & René Maingnon Salmeron

Agua Amarga is one of the most attractive of Almería's coastal villages. People know about the place and in summer you won't have the beach to yourself. But its still a great place to kick back. René and Michèle Salmeron first came here on holiday and were so taken by the village that they upped sticks and moved south to open this unassuming little hostal. The position is perfect, a couple of hundred yards from the village on the far bank of the (dry) river that cuts down from the hills. The Family's restaurant has become an obligatory stopover for many of the inland ex-pat community when they come for a day by the sea. Michèle cooks well and the huge portions have no hint of nouvelle cuisine. Her specialities include duck à l'orange, wild boar and stuffed tomatoes. All meals are accompanied by heaps of good vegetables and taped music (eg Elton John). The dining room looks out to the swimming pool as do the bedrooms. The nicest are those that have recently been built on top of the original edifice. The Family has no airs of grandeur but its rooms are light, clean and comfortable.

To see and do: walking, beaches, the scuba diving school in Agua Amarga, the Cabo de Gata Park, the village of Nijar.

CORTIJO EL NACIMIENTO

4639 Turre   **Map: 15**
(Almería)

Tel: 950 528090

Closed: November.

Bedrooms: 4 Doubles & 1 Twin.

Prices: Double/Twin €33 (5500 Ptas).

Meals: Breakfast included, Dinner €9 (1400 Ptas) including wine.

Getting there: from the N-340/E-15 take exit 520 towards Turre/ Mojácar. After 3km turn right into the entrance of Cortijo Grande. Continue towards Cabrera for exactly 4.9km and then turn right on to dirt road (signposted here).

107

Management: Adolfo & María Valdés

Most people who head up into the Cabrera mountains are
bound for Cortijo Grande. This amazing collection of luxurious,
hilltop villas was the brainchild of an English architect who also
had the whacky idea of converting the gardens of a Moorish
palace into two full-sized crown bowling greens! Cortijo El
Nacimiento has an altogether different feel. Adolfo and María
are a friendly Spanish couple who headed for the hills in search
of the Good Life, and for the last 9 years have welcomed guests
to this 200-year-old rambling farm house. This is the complete
antithesis of the chain hotel and might not be to everyone's
taste. You swim in a deep pool where the river's been dammed,
bedrooms are reached via creaking stairs where bathrooms
might be separated by just a curtain, vegetarian suppers (many
of the ingredients organically grown in María's vegetable
garden) are served round one large table where the lingua
franca may well be Spanish. This is a place with masses of
personality, no airs of grandeur and anybody with vaguely eco
leanings will love it.

To see and do: walking in the hills surrounding the farm, horse-
riding at a nearby farm, the village of Mojácar.

FINCA LISTONERO

Cortijo Grande   **Map: 15**
4639 Turre
(Almería)

Tel: 950 479094   **Fax:** 950 479094

Closed: Never.

Bedrooms: 1 Double and 4 Twins.

Prices: Double/Twin €72–84 (12000–14000 Ptas) + 7% TAX.

Meals: Breakfast included, Lunch (snacks only), Dinner €27 (4500 Ptas) excluding drinks. Restaurant closed on Sunday nights.

Getting there: from the N-340/E-15 take exit 520 towards Turre/Mojácar. After 3km turn right into the entrance of Cortijo Grande. Continue towards Cortijo Cabrera and Listonero is signposted on the right after 3.5km.

108

Management: Graeme Gibson & David Rice

David and Graham might be known to some readers living on the Costa del Sol. They used to run the Yellow Book restaurant in Estepona. After a brief period in Australia, they returned to southern Spain, this time to the mountains of Almería, where they have set up another marvellous restaurant which doubles as a country-house hotel. The food is to write home about. David is in charge of things culinary and his cuisine is gourmet, flavoursome and beautifully presented. Meals tend to begin with an aperitif in Listonero's lounge, which is decorated in a soothing cool peppermint and is particularly memorable at night when its several lamps and candles are lit. The mood is romantic, relaxing and intimate. The bedrooms (choose between the pink, yellow, green or blue depending on your mood) are just as appealing and are set around a shaded patio whose salmon pink colour provides a beautiful contrast to all of the greenery. A convivial, house-party atmosphere is guaranteed should you stay at Listonero and there's a wonderful pool sculpted into the mountainside just beneath the house.

To see and do: beaches, walking in the Cabo de Gata Park, the village of Mojácar, Mini Hollywood where spaghetti westerns were filmed.

CASA GEMINIS

Ctra Mojácar-Turre   **Map: 15**
4638 Mojácar
(Almería)

Tel: 950 478013

e-mail: geha@computronx.com

Web Page:

Closed: Never.

Bedrooms: 1 Double & 1 Twin.

Prices: Double/Twin €48–60 (8000–10000 Ptas) including TAX.

Meals: Breakfast included, Lunch/Dinner €18 (3000 Ptas) including wine.

Getting there: from N-340 take exit 520 for Los Gallardos/Turre/ Mojácar. Go through Turre and continue towards Mojácar for 3kms. Just after a sharp S-bend Casa Geminis is on the right, just before the Delfos restaurant.

109

Management: Eileen & Geoff Howard-Ady

Eileen worked in television, Geoff as a location caterer for film companies (they met on the set of "London's burning") before they moved south to Almería to set up this small B&B. Casa Geminis is just a mile or so from Mojácar. This picture-postcard village is still worth a detour but nowadays you'd do best to visit later in the day by which time the day-trippers have moved on. Your hosts are exceptionally sociable and really do seem to take pleasure in sharing their home with guests. Thanks to the exceptional climate of this area, most of the year life is lived around the pool where Geoff sets up a marquee which serves as dining room and bar. Be sure to book dinner if you stay with the Howard-Adys: Geoff really loves to cook and amongst his most popular dishes are suckling pig and "a mean paella". Wine and conversation flows freely and the mood is easy and relaxed. The two guest rooms come equipped with every imaginable extra (fridge, hairdryer, teasmade, bathrobes) and they are kept cool by whirling Casablanca-type fans.

To see and do: the market, marina and castle in Águilas, Mini Hollywood film set at Sorbas, the Cabo de Gata Natural Park.

HOTEL TIKAR

Ctra Garrucha a Vera s/n   **Map: 15**
4630 Garrucha
(Almería)

Tel: 950 617131   **Fax:** 950 617132

e-mail: hotel@nexo.es

Web Page: www.hoteltikar.com

Closed: November.

Bedrooms: 1 Double & 5 Twins.

Prices: Double/Twin €48 (8000 Ptas) + 7% TAX.

Meals: Breakfast €3 (500 Ptas), Lunch & Dinner €15 (2500 Ptas) excluding wine.

Getting there: from the N-340 take exit 534 for Garrucha. Continue past Vera and then on round Garrucha. At roundabout continue straight on and the hotel is on your right.

110

Management: Beatriz Gallego & Sean McMahon

Sean, Beatriz and their young son Diego have stamped their personality on this small, modern restaurant and hotel (it's easy to spot its gay blue and white facade as you leave Garrucha) and it is already making big waves amongst the local ex-pat community. The decoration of the lounge and restaurant is a wonderfully orchestrated mix of dark parquet, burnt orange and blue ragged walls, elegant teak chairs and modern art (the hotel doubles as an exhibition space for young artists). The food is just as cosmopolitan, the sort of fare you might get in one of California's diners – fresh vegetables, light sauces, a high salad content and the best cuts of meat. The wine list is just as interesting, not just Riojas and Riberas but also good bottles from Chile, Argentina, South Africa or France. And although this is, to quote Sean, "a restaurant with rooms," you'll stay in a large, beautifully designed and decorated bedroom whose level of comfort is amazing given their price. Beatriz and Sean are the nicest hosts and, believe me, theirs is one of the most special small hotels around.

To see and do: colourful evening fish auction in Garrucha, scuba diving and other watersports, riding and walking in the Cabrera mountains.

LOS SIBILEYS

Nogalte 84   **Map: 15**
30800 Lorca
(Almería/Murcia)

Tel: 968 439024 or 626 955346   **Fax:** 968 439024

Web Page: www.andalucia.com/accommodation/lossibileys/ home.htm

Closed: Never.

Bedrooms: 2 Doubles & 3 Twins.

Prices: Double/Twin €60 (10000 Ptas) including TAX.

Meals: Breakfast included, Lunch - tapas/snacks €6 (1000 Ptas), Dinner €21 (3500 Ptas) excluding wine.

Getting there: from P. Lumbreras west on N-342 then exit 93 for Henares. At small roundabout take second exit for "Servicios". Pass petrol station and after 1.5km left over motorway to roundabout. Here take last exit and after 100m turn right at sign "Camino de la Venta de la Petra a Nogalte." 3km track to the house.

111

Management: Judith & Karl Lanchbury

Hacienda de Los Sibileys is right on the easternmost border of Andalucía, an isolated farmhouse in the midst of an amazing multicoloured landscape of ochre, terracotta and burned sienna, all of it softened and brought to life by groves of olive and almonds. It's easy to see why the area is attracting more and more ex-pats in search of their Arcadia-in-the-sun. The Lanchburys were amongst the first to arrive and have chosen a blissfully isolated, tranquil spot to build the guest house of their dreams. Having chartered yachts for many years, Karl must be accustomed to confined quarters but things have been built on a generous scale at Los Sibileys. The guest rooms are big with attractive Mexican furniture and the most comfortable of beds. The same spacious feel is apparent in the lounge and dining room where there lots of the prints and oils with a nautical theme. I thoroughly enjoyed Judith's cooking (she'll happily prepare you a light tapas lunch if you are tempted to laze by the pool), Karl's choice of wine and the kindness of them both.

To see and do: horse-riding, ornithology, the Saturday market in Vélez Rubio, the Moorish castle and Letreros cave (with paleaolithic art) in Vélez Rubio.

GLOSSARY

alvaro	a deep ochre colour - that of the sand in the bullring
aril	a light blue colour with a hint of purple
barranco	a deep sided gorge, typical of La Alpujarra
chocolate	hot chocolate, essential to accompany 'churros'
churros	long, thin do-nuts, best accompanied by 'chocolate'
cortijo	a farm: can be large, medium-sized or small
degustacion	a tasting - of wine, cheese, olive oil etc
fino	dry sherry
hammam	arabic term for a bath house
hostal	a simple inn
huerta	an irrigated plot of land or allotment
judería	the Jewish quarter
latifundio	a very large estate
levante	a hot, dry wind that blows hard from the East
lomo	loin (nearly always of pork)
manzanilla	similar to fino but from the area round Sanlucar
matanza	the slaughter and preparation of a pig
mudejar	Moorish style of architecture but post-conquest
palacete	a grand country of towm mansion house
posada	a small village/country hotel (orig. coaching inn)
rejas	wrought-iron window/door grille
tapa	a small plate of food served with an aperitif

USEFUL PHONE NUMBERS

Almeria	Tourist office	950 274355
	Guardia Civil	950 256122
	Renfe (trains)	902 240202
Cadiz	Tourist office	956 211313
	Guardia Civil	956 253370
	Renfe (trains)	902 240202
Cordoba	Tourist office	957 200522
	Guardia Civil	957 414800
	Renfe (trains)	902 240202
Granada	Tourist office	958 225990
	Guardia Civil	958 185400
	Renfe (trains)	902 240202
	Alhambra (tickets)	902 224460
Huelva	Tourist office	959 257403
	Guardia Civil	959 241900
	Renfe (trains)	902 240202
Jaen	Tourist office	953 222737
	Guardia Civil	953 250340
	Renfe (trains)	902 240202
Malaga	Tourist office	95 2213445
	Guardia Civil	95 2071520
	Renfe (trains)	902 240202
Sevilla	Tourist office	95 4221404
	Guardia Civil	95 4231902
	Renfe (trains)	902 240202
Weather Info (in Spanish)		906 365329
Directory Enquiries		1003
International Enquiries		025

YOUR OPINIONS

Please let us know about your experiences at the places that we include in this book. And please let us know about any good places that you discover which aren't included in this guide.

NAME of HOTEL: ....

Date of visit: ....

Your comments: ....
....
....
....

Your opinion of the food & wine: ....
....
....
....

Your name: ....

Address: ....
....

Contact number: ....
(if you are happy to give us these details).

Please send by post to: Guy Hunter-Watts
                            El Tejar, 29430 Montecorto
                            Málaga.

By fax to: (00 34) 95 2184053

Or by e-mail to: guyhw@mercuryin.es

Many thanks.